The Premium Schools

An Abridged Story of Nigerian Heritage Secondary Schools

Seye Adetunmbi

The Premium Schools

Premium Schools in Nigeria
© 2022, Seye Adetunmbi

1st Edition 2022

ISBN: 9798841248125

Cover Design Concept and Contents Layout by: Seye Adetunmbi

Published by
MINDSCOPE AFRICA
Northfleet, Gravesend
Kent
England
mindscopeafrica@gmail.com

DEDICATION

This book is dedicated to the memory of those who founded early schools in Nigeria and devoted their time, energy and financial resources to grow the secondary schools to prized heritages they have become today. Also, to the various alumni who have committed their resources and integrated goodwill to sustain the legacy and the glory of the secondary schools they attended.

"Life is a staircase where we can only recall about steps backward but we only have to reach forward."
Srinivas Mishra

"There is life in walking, but death in running - there is life in communication, but death in talking - there is life in awareness, but death in judgement - so, be the life my friend, without the judgement, without the talking, without the running - simply be the life, full with sparkling communications, revelatory awareness and heart-warming walks." -
Abhijit Naskar

"Let your mind start a journey through a strange new world. Leave all thoughts of the world you knew before. Let your soul take you where you long to be…Close your eyes let your spirit start to soar, and you'll live as you've never lived before. – **Erich Fromm**

"Begin doing what you want to do now.
We are not living in eternity. We have only this moment, sparkling like a star in our hand and melting like a snowflake. Let us use it before it is too late."
Marie Beynon Lyons Ray

"Who you were, who you are, and
who you become, are all different people."
DP Sayings.Com

CONTENTS

		Page
Dedication		3
Preface		7
Prologue		13

Part I

1.	The Last Quarter of the 19th Century	19
2.	The First Two Decades in the 20th Century	29
3.	Schools Founded Between 1920 and 1930	39
4.	The Schools Established in 1931 to 1940	49
5.	The 4th Decade in the 20th Century: 1941-1950	75
6.	Fifth Decade in the 20th Century: 1951-1960	83
7.	The 1960s Secondary Schools in Nigeria	97
8.	The New Generation Heritage Schools	111

Part II

9.	The Grammar School	117
9.1.	Ifaki Grammar School Heritage: An Overview of 1957-2022	118
9.2.	Ifaki Grammar School Culture, Traditions and Integrated Reminisces	124

Part III

10.	Reminiscences of Products of Old Generation Schools	137
10.1.	Aquinas College, Akure	137
10.2.	Christ's School, Ado-Ekiti	138
10.3.	Ifaki Grammar School	164
Epilogue		175
Annex:	A Directory of old Generation Secondary Schools in Nigeria 1885-1973	179
Appendix:	Graphical Illustrations	185
Acknowledgments		189
Index		190
About the Author		196

"A hero is born among a hundred, a wise man is found among a thousand,
but an accomplished one might not be found even among a hundred thousand men."
Plato

"Life has a tendency to provide a person with what they need in order to grow. Our beliefs, what we value in life, provide the roadmap for the type of life that we experience. A period of personal unhappiness reveals that our values are misplaced and we are on the wrong path. Unless a person changes their values and ideas, they will continue to experience discontentment."
Killjoy J. Old Ster

"It's all connected. Your gifts, your circumstances, your purpose, your imperfections, your journey, your destiny. It's moulding you. Embrace it."
Emperor Haile Selassie (Ras Tafari)

"It's your road and yours alone, others may walk it with you, but no one can walk it for you."
RUMI

It's a journey. No one is ahead of you or behind you. You are not more "advanced" or less enlightened. You are exactly where you need to be. It's not a contest. It's life. We are all teachers and we are all students."
Billy Carson

"We can easily forgive a child who is afraid of the dark; the real tragedy of life is when men are afraid of the light."
Plato

PREFACE

This book, **The Premium Schools** (TPS) in Nigeria, is yet another unusual book from the series of my published books, since year 2012 till date. It was feedbacks that I got from people who have read my articles and books that encouraged me to write more. Extracts of blurbs on some of my published books are quoted in this preface for ease of reference and as a prelude to this book, for the pleasurable reading of the readers. Essentially, the quotes humbly introduce me to those reading my book for the first time and whet the imagination of readers on what to expect in this book in terms of facts, information, illustration and pictorial presentation.

Abridged Biographies and Integrated Panegyric (2022)

"I have read every word of your book. Between all the lines and in every word, I see commitment and perseverance. I cannot help but wonder how much better our country would be if more Nigerians had your inspired vision and patriotism. I have no doubt in my mind that the book will be a great asset to the nation and a source of inspiration to its youth and politicians alike including all that come across it. As for me who has always been guided by the examples of great achievers, reading through the book gave me additional inspiration. May the almighty God continue to keep and bless you for your efforts and contributions" – **Chief Olusegun Obasanjo**

"It is an encyclopaedia bringing the world under one roof! It is a challenge to human industry to write in such minute details and in such elevated diction with the most inevitable words. Seye, this is a legacy for time and eternity. Each biography is told in the three dimensions of the subject. This is unique. As I started reading through the book, I went on nonstop for ten hours! The book encapsulates a world panorama. It is a treasure and a gift to our age." - Nonagenarian **High Chief Alex Ajayi**, the Odoba of Ado-Ekiti

Octogenarian **Venerable L. L. Eso** wrote: "Seye, this is awesome. One of its kind…..could only have come from Adetunmbi's stable. Brilliant and legendary! That is what it will always represent! Congratulations……….keep on flying like the eagle…"

"Oh, dear Seye, That's a Great One and Quite Unique.." - **Yemi Akeju**

The nonagenarian **Chief (Dr.) Francis Adebayo Daramola** wrote: "Congratulations on the publication of the 'Abridged Biographies and Integrated

Panegyrics'. I see the work as an encyclopaedia of the 'greats' the 'nobles', men and women role models who have contributed immensely to society and societal life at not only local level, but at national and international levels of human engineering and endeavour. I feel honoured and relished to see write-ups on some of my teachers, my old classmates…all of whom are alumni of the prestigious Christ's School, Ado-Ekiti among those featured in the scholarly biographies. There are others I know who have made names in the military, academia, medicine, the world of commerce and industry etc. The pictures that adorn the "Abridged Biographies and Integrated Panegyrics" are of rich and illuminating quality. The book is a "must read" for old and young and should be found in libraries and book shelves, more so now that the study of History is being given priority in our institutions and school curriculum. Well-done Seye, *omo Baba*. May your tribe increase.

Dotun Akinola wrote: The book is lovely. Thank you so much for honouring my father. Words cannot express my gratitude. I will be showing this to everyone who visits me now!

Applied Knowledge and Lateral Thinking (2021)

"…I don't know how you do these things - work hard, religion, socialise, politics and write. Well done. 6/8/21 I'm amazed at how you deploy your energy at various projects with such ease.... I commend your efforts". - **Chief Dr Biodun Shobanjo**, Advertising Guru, 9/12/2021

Christianity and Anglicanism (2020)

"I cannot but express my delight in having the singular privilege of writing the foreword to this justifiable literary effort by Seye Adetunmbi, in defence of the Christian faith and our own cherished Anglican heritage. Being son of a Church prelate notwithstanding, his display of interest and knowledge of the foundation of the Christian faith vis-a-vis the historic formulary of the Church is quite interesting and commendable…." - **Rt. Rev James Olusola Odedeji,** *The Lord Bishop, Diocese of Lagos West*, 9/9/2020

"The handbook for believers in Christian faith epitomizes a unique learning experience, shaped in six sections, with annexes, index…The book is a product of a background of remarkable experiences to underscore the fact that God works in a mysterious way. The book is written to foster a deeper understanding of Biblical truth, History, Doctrine, Christianity, and the Church, etc. in a world where Christianity is misunderstood – and often dented-by people, powers, and forces that shape modern-day society. This book is for the equipping of the Saints Militant.........We thank Seye

Adetunmbi for yielding himself to God for this timely, unique, great, and godly work of the moment. - **Rt. Rev. Isaac Olubowale**, *The Lord Bishop, Diocese of Ekiti-Oke*, 13/9/2020

"Seye Adetunmbi is becoming a rather consistent writer; he writes with a versatility of themes and topics. Right on the heels of his book on the Nigerian capital market still basking in its recent launch, he added this refreshing book on religion to his growing intellectual stable. The is both evidence-based and anecdotal. It profiles the history, character and nomenclatures in the Church of Nigeria in a wide aperture literature mixed with throw backs to the author's father and family's commitment as dedicated Churchmen, and the author's personal, spiritual and career growth. Son of a Scion and dedicated Church Organist, Seye himself has self-consciously developed into a well-rounded personality, adroitly blending a career in the Nigerian finance sector with deepening spirituality and active service as a niche Churchman. The book stands gallantly upon the shoulders of time and opens the window for more intellectual, spiritual and policy discourse on the pathway that Christianity and Anglicanism must thread for survival and viability" **Ven. Segun Agbetuyi**, 14/9/2020

...........I like much of what I see particularly your interrogative style on the commandments and the beatitudes. A very good way of teaching. - **Rt. Rev. Peter Bryan Price**, Southwark Diocese, London 3/7/22

Financial Intermediation and Practice (2020)

"...I am glad I wrote the foreword to the book which I read in-to-to. It is a combination of theory, practice and history of the capital market. I commend him for having the courage and commitment to do this. I am proud to be associated with the book" - **Atedo Peterside**, *Founder of IBTC,* 21/7/2020

"It is a timely book, coming out, post the unprecedented global crisis. The book will enable regulators, market participants, issuers, investors - retail and institutional investors to understand better the jewels and gems of the market. The book can help to truly unleash the potential of our market. It is a book written by a veteran investment banker and stockbroker who understands the Nigerian economy from his wealth of experience garnered...He is a candid commentator on the Nigerian economy. A role model worthy of emulation for his humility, sense of community...Thank you for your service to the nation through the capital market, also through your writings that extend beyond the capital market; it covers culture, Nigerian economy, history and politics; you illuminate Nigeria for people within and outside world to appreciate. I look forward to a nation and society that will continue to benefit from your intellect and commitment to showcasing Nigerian capital market in Nigeria and Africa." **Arunma Oteh**, *former Director-General of the Nigeria Securities &Exchange Commission (*SEC)*, 21/7/2020*

"I am really impressed with what I have read in the book, it is a major contribution to the capital market Nigeria. I particularly like the section on securitisation because we have a lot of huge assets that can be securitized." – **Lamido Yuguda**, *Director-General of* SEC, 21/7/2020

"The book will fill a lot of vacuums that exist when we talk of the capital market in Nigeria. Very apt that such experiences are documented in a book that many generations yet unborn will yet meet and find useful" - **Oscar Onyema**, *Group* CEO, *Nigerian Stock Exchange, 21/7/2020*

"It is an excellently punctuated book, a great work in academic exercise and would be a wonderful addition to anyone's library."- **Bola Ajomale**, *Managing Director of National Association of Securities Dealers PLC, 21/7/20*

...I have always admired your bullish peculiarities.... **Chief Dele Fajemirokun**, a distinguished and successful entrepreneur, 27/6/2020

"The book is a useful compendium for financial market operators, capital market professionals, and university students. It will also serve investors, portfolio managers, college professors, and government functionaries in the pursuit of financial knowledge and understanding." - **Tayo Shenbanjo**, *Licensed Financial Advisor, USA, 3/7/2020*

The Apostle of Harmony (2018)

"I must commend you for documenting what Chief Adetunmbi stood for and how he impacted the society through his glorious teaching career and his other endeavours. I found the book highly insightful; it reveals his active involvement in unionism, where he rose to become a national leader of Nigerian Union of Teachers and in community service'' **Senator Ibikunle Amosun**, 6/10/2021

Ekitipanupo Legacy Book: Published in 2015

"You are, apart from your professional expertise, too many things rolled into one: an essayist, an historian, a literary artist, an activist, a journalist, a critic, an organizer, a mobilizer etc...You are such an impresario! - **Professor Samuel Ade Ojo**

"You are deep in upbringing and you have in addition, "given yourself a rebirth". No doubt you have created a niche for yourself" – **Prof J. F. Olorunfemi**

10

"I value the adventurous energy of Seye Adetunmbi who, from now on, I will be calling the People-Gatherer" - **Professor Niyi Osundare** a reknowned poet

Mindset: Published in 2012

"The compendium has added a unique contribution to the growing literature on the proverbial question of "Whither Nigeria?"...The author succeeded in making his work partly biographical, technical and partly historical, thereby rendering it as one of enduring value and relevance, especially to this and successive generations...Every one of us has a definite mindset, informed and shaped by a Welt Anschauung or world-view. Seye Adetunmbi has, through this book, exhibited his own window to the world" - **Professor Akin Oyebode,** 1/7/2012

"An amazing effort...You are obviously the linchpin - the 'non pareil'" - **Dr Femi Orebe,** 2012

This book, TPS is equally loaded in essence, and quite rich in contents. It is historical and the contents were well researched with some vintage pictures supporting the stories. Information and facts of the schools written about here, including some of the photos, were sourced on the internet, also through old students, past and present teachers and principals of the schools.

Few selected philosophical quotes were included in this publication; primarily used, to inspire readers and to plan the pages while flipping through the book. It is my hope that everyone who gets a copy of the book will find it interesting to read and your feedback will be appreciated. It will help to improve on the subsequent editions.

It is in my humble nature to associate something of substance with the celebration of milestones in my life. For an example, my first published book, MINDSET, was formally presented to the public on the 21st of July in 2012 to mark my 50th birthday anniversary. Consequently, to appreciate God for the privilege of marking diamond age milestone in good health, I ensured, through the grace of God, that I got this book ready before my 60th birthday anniversary. To the glory of God, this book got to Amazon shelf on scheduled and was formally presented to the public, on the 21st of July in 2022, my birthday anniversary.

Let me state here that the narratives in this book do not cover all the schools within the first 100 years of the debut of secondary schools in Nigeria, nor tell all the stories. However, there is a directive of secondary schools between 1885 and 1973 in the annex. It doesn't matter if anyone who reads this book is a product of any of the schools written about here, or the school that a reader attended was not captured in the book; yet, there is something for everybody. In one way or the other, there is likelihood of the fact that most of the readers would have one link or the other with one or more of the premium schools through parents, uncles, aunties, siblings, cousins, friends, colleagues or other associates. Also, every picture of an alumnus or alumna used under each school is a representative symbol of the numerous excellent products of the schools that cannot all be accommodated in a book. The modest work done here is based on available information in the public domain, provided materials in some quarters and the whole package was moderated by limited space for publication, no omission intended, please pardon any mistake.

There is no way that this kind of book will satisfy everybody. While taking responsibility for the contents of this maiden edition, it provides an opportunity for any interested researcher to improve on this humble effort by filling necessary gaps and make the published book available to the reading public. It is also hoped that this book will encourage others to tell their story too. Nevertheless, this is yet another good book to enrich the library of anyone who reads and appreciates a well-researched and diligently illustrated book, or needs a readily available basic historical information on the secondary schools in Nigeria, from the 19th century to the 21st century. It is available online, through Amazon, irrespective of your location, globally.

I wish everyone who gets a copy a refreshing reading.

Seye Adetunmbi
21/7/22

PROLOGUE

Sometime in 2017, a list of the early set of secondary schools in Nigeria was circulated on the social media. While going through the list, I noticed that some schools were omitted and I took it upon myself to update the list and share with the various interactive e-forums that I initiated. My updated list further generated more interests among old students of the listed schools. Those whose schools were left out, called my attention to it and I updated the list of the schools accordingly. In the end, I was able to compile a list of over 100 secondary schools in Nigeria from 1855-1965. Apparently, there was no central accurate data base of all the secondary schools covering the period being written about here that can be pulled out as one consolidated document or file, for ease of reference. There and then, I decided to write a book around the list such that as many interested people as possible can have access to a one-stop book on the heritage and premium schools in Nigeria. It is my hope that my attention will be called to any school that has been left out in the directory available in this book, for consideration in the subsequent editions.

Considering the fact that I have written a book about Christ's School, Ado-Ekiti THE SCHOOL: A Compendium on Christ's School (Mindscope): Adetunmbi, Seye: 9789789797288: Amazon.com: Books which I attended for Higher School Certificate Course in 1979 to 1981, some of my fellow school mates in 1973 to 1978 at Ifaki Grammar School (IGS), kept asking me: "when would I write about our alma mater, too"? This is why I decided to write about the early secondary schools in Nigeria and the second section of the book is dedicated to tell the story of IGS as documented by me over the years, being a school my beloved father, Chief D. O. Adetunmbi (1919-1990) Amazon.com: The Apostle of Harmony: The Biography of Chief D.O. Adetunmbi 1919-1990: 9789789444069: Adetunmbi, Seye: Books laboured to build as one of the founding teachers and administrators from the scratch in 1957.

Consequently, this is yet another historical book from me; it contains an abridged history of most of the early remarkable secondary schools in Nigeria from 1855 to 1965 primarily; and by extension, an overview of the frontline new generation premium schools in Nigeria founded up till the 21st century. At the same time, the book lists out the heritage secondary schools in Nigeria based on available records. Understandably, there are more features on Christ's School, Ado-Ekiti and Ifaki Grammar School, Ifaki-Ekiti because I am a product of the two heritage schools and I have done an extensive research on them earlier which made the highlights on them here very rich in contents.

Historically, few of the early heritage schools started as a primary school. The Lagos Baptist Academy for an example was established in 1855 as a primary school. By1886, the school had about 129 boys and 95 girls in the primary section and about 14 boys and 3 girls in the secondary section. This may be the transition of the school to a secondary school. Likewise, Christ's School, Ado-Ekiti that was founded by Venerable Archdeacon Henry Dallimore, started as a primary school in 1933 and graduated to a secondary school in 1940. CMS Grammar School in Bariga, Lagos started in 1859 as a secondary school in the Nigeria and the delighted old students would always describe their alma mater as the primus inter pares amongst others.

Published reports on the census in Nigeria reveal that in 1921, there are 51 government schools, 139 assisted schools, 2,053 non-assisted schools and 137,235 have been to school which was like 1.5% of the population in the southern part of the country then. The 1931 census highlighted 176 government schools, 291 assisted schools, 2,771 non-assisted Christian schools, 33,426 muslim schools and 378,543 in school, which constituted 1.9% of the population in the northern and southern part of the country. The census of 1956 classified 2,568,381 Nigerians, 8.24% of the population as having some kind of education.

There are also links between the development of education in Nigeria with the slave trade, with the religion missions and the colonial government. For instance, some of the early educated Nigerians were descendants of exported slaves and the released latter day slaves who played some pioneering roles in the planting of primary and secondary education in southern part of Nigeria. Also, the missionary bodies took their turns to make inroads to the spiritual minds of the people through the establishment of elementary and secondary schools, most of which have become huge heritages till date.

Of course, the colonial governments relatively had their fears in educating indigenes of their colonies. Patterns of colonial education revealed that small investments in education were made by colonial powers which had important effects on the social mobility and political engagement. Africans predominantly demanded more Western education, while the colonial powers feared that education would threaten their control, so primary education remained scarce and secondary education essentially non-existent. Both the French and the British colonial administrators were especially wary of secondary education.

For an example as at 1939, there was no secondary education available in the Central Africa. The first secondary school in French Equatorial Africa was founded in Brazzaville in 1935. Educational policy was based on a pyramidal system, whereby the primary education was expanding but severely restricting access to secondary education. (*See Appendix I.*)

According to Huillery in 2009, education in the French colony was financed entirely by colonies with no contributions from metropole. Investment tended to concentrate over time as marginal investments flowed to areas with existing facilities and locally, high demand for education (which, in turn, was fueled by earlier investments in education). Low level of investment made in education through grants to missionary schools. In turn, missionary schools were generally run on the initiative of Africans. For an example, at Uganda in 1938, 8,456 African teachers taught in the primary schools, while there were only 285 European teachers according to Frankema in 2012. Larger investments were evidently made in the coastal areas. Despite the existence of matriarchal traditions in many parts of pre-colonial Africa, colonial education for women was most severely limited.

Nevertheless, the colonial government in Nigeria did their bit in the establishment of schools e.g. King's College, Lagos and Queen's Colleges. Southern Nigeria had one of the most developed secondary education systems in Sub-Saharan Africa. The vast majority of these were missionary schools, with limited support from the colonial state. Post-independence governments, established federal government colleges; while some communities started establishing schools when the colonial schools couldn't go round satisfactorily. Ekiti Parapo College in Ido-Ekiti, that was established in 1954, is an example of a secondary school established by a progressive ethnic group in diaspora. In essence, Nigeria is multi institutional in the context of national and ethnic based institutions. Ethnic based institutions vary across many different characteristics while interactions between ethnicity-based and colonial institutions resulted in the complex mosaic outcomes in the education sector, which continue to have some relevance till today.

Coming to curriculum in African schools, the more practical and rudimentary the education is, the better and more useful schools would be. For instance, the adapted curriculum by Camille Guy, the Lieutenant Governor of Senegal in 1903, referred to the idea that the black communities required less advanced syllabus, but more localized education which was separate from the European education. His presentation in 1941 titled: How Shall We Educate the Africans, introduced the need for African anthropology, ethnology, and ethnography in secondary and collegiate education. He posited that African educators should focus on the social sciences whilst providing necessary agricultural and industrial education.

Azikiwe stressed that technical/vocational training should be emphasized to the extent that "Africans are educated as human beings and not museum specimen or a fossil or preserved animal for scientific experimentation." According to Frankema in 2012, the British colonies gave grants to private missionary schools rather than investing in public education systems. Likewise, Ball in 1983 and Zvogbo in 1981 stated that grants were contingent on mission schools providing vocational training alone. In practice invariably, students spent most of their days in indentured labor with no real education going on in schools.

With relation to regional disparities and persistence of northern and southern Nigeria in 1914, the northern Nigeria had eight primary school, two technical government schools, 512 total pupils. Southern Nigeria had 541 primary schools, out of which 487 were mission schools with 65,000 total pupils as published in the Annual Report of the Colonies. By 1952, the school enrollment increased to 900,000/2.35 million children in the Northern Nigeria and 120,000/2.5 million children in Southern Nigeria. Expectedly, the figures have been increasing since then till date, as a result of the growing population and integrated interventions of various governments in Nigeria through Universal Primary Education (UPE) that was launched in 1955, UBE and SUBEB schemes

Quoting from "The Nigerian education system: Past Present and Future", the book by C. O. Taiwo, published in 1982, expansion grew in the primary school enrolment from 465,600 in 1954, a year before free UPE was launched, to 811,432 in 1955. By 1959, there were 1,080,303 pupils in the primary schools. In 1954 there were 3,550 primary schools, but in 1955, the number of primary schools had risen to 6,407, this constituted over 90% increase. The phenomenal rise in the number of pupils in the primary schools in 1955, of 811,432 as against 456,600 in 1954 represented an increase from 35% to 61% of the 5 to14 years old. Of course, increase in the enrolment to the secondary schools was expected to follow suit. The enrolments rose from 9,126 pupils in 1954, to 22,374 in 1959.

The sad narrative today, of the heritage schools that most people wished to attend in the olden days is that, most of them have become a shadow of themselves, due to poor and irresponsible government that took over management of the schools over the years. A few of the schools have lost out either by being de-established or their original school site had been taken over by government, for a different scheme and the legacy went down the drain. Some lucky ones are being salvaged through the concerted efforts of the old students' associations and missions that their earlier taken-over schools have been returned to them.

The essence of this book is to highlight the history of those good schools with unique heritages. Also, to document how they were managed to produce the best of human capital and a unique league of various distinguished personalities, technocrats and top-notch professionals that Nigeria has ever been blessed with in the pre-colonial days till date. This will enable those committed to restoration in the heritage schools, to know what to do to bring back the lost glories of the once upon a time premium schools in Nigeria.

Premium institutions in the context of this book are the secondary schools that paraded lasting values, culture and traditions over the years which in turn resulted to their students standing out in academics, sports and other extra-curricular activities. Every institution attended by people may amount to a kind of heritage to those who passed through such secondary school, but not every school is a premium, especially when compared to others based on some universally acceptable standards.

Nostalgically, the government and missionary schools of old, were predominantly the premium schools then. It was a leveller for the children and wards of the money bags, president, the parliamentarians, governors, other top government officials/senior civil servants, and all other ranks of the working class including some artisans and peasants who can meet the basic sponsorship requirements. Yes, children of the high, middle and low attended same school. Private schools were never the first choice of parents and students because, most of them then could not match standard of the public and missionary schools in terms of infrastructures, qualified teachers, quality of admitted students etc. As a matter of fact, it was when a place could not be secured in the good schools of old that people opted for available private schools. The reverse is the case these days with the takeover by the new generation premium private secondary schools in Nigeria, at a high cost to parents who send their children there. The situation is so bad today that not many people who can afford good private schools would gladly send their children to the secondary schools they attended, with pride.

This book nonetheless, tells the story of the schools that brought so much joy to their products, focussing more on those values that made their alma mater to be so dear to them. However, the book also serves as a directory of secondary schools in Nigeria within the covered area of study for the perusal of anyone who is interested, for ease of reference.

SECTION ONE

Highlights on Secondary Schools in Nigeria in 1855-1985

CHAPTER ONE

THE LAST QUARTER OF THE 19TH CENTURY

1.1. BAPTIST ACADEMY, OBANIKORO, LAGOS

This is the oldest formal school in Nigeria, historically. The Baptist Academy which started as a primary school in 1855, was founded by the American Baptist Missionaries who were behind the establishment of the First Baptist Church Mission in Lagos. Oba Dosunmu gave the mission a parcel of land on which the school structures were built and educational activities started after the completion of the buildings. The school started on the Broad Street in Lagos-Island and later moved to the permanent site at Obanikoro, along the Ikorodu Road in Lagos. The primary school was renamed William Joshua David Memorial Baptist Primary School. It was named after one of the American Baptist missionaries who started the Baptist Mission in Nigeria. The primary school remained at the Broad Street location until the late nineteen eighties when its building was pulled down in anticipation of expanding the First Baptist Church, that stands adjacent to the school, in order to include a high-rise business building. All the students at W. J. David were transferred to other Baptist primary schools in the area.

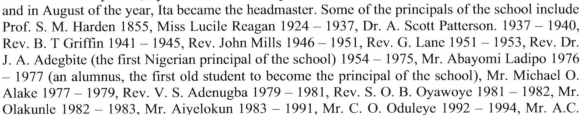

By 1886, the school had about 129 boys and 95 girls in the primary section and about 14 boys and 3 girls in the secondary section. Until 1926, American pastors of the Baptist Mission acted as the principals for the school. In January 1926, Eyo Ita and E. E. Esua joined the staff of the school and in August of the year, Ita became the headmaster. Some of the principals of the school include Prof. S. M. Harden 1855, Miss Lucile Reagan 1924 – 1937, Dr. A. Scott Patterson. 1937 – 1940, Rev. B. T Griffin 1941 – 1945, Rev. John Mills 1946 – 1951, Rev. G. Lane 1951 – 1953, Rev. Dr. J. A. Adegbite (the first Nigerian principal of the school) 1954 – 1975, Mr. Abayomi Ladipo 1976 – 1977 (an alumnus, the first old student to become the principal of the school), Mr. Michael O. Alake 1977 – 1979, Rev. V. S. Adenugba 1979 – 1981, Rev. S. O. B. Oyawoye 1981 – 1982, Mr. Olakunle 1982 – 1983, Mr. Aiyelokun 1983 – 1991, Mr. C. O. Oduleye 1992 – 1994, Mr. A.C.

Adesanya. 1994 – 1999, Mrs. F.O. Ojo. 1999 – 2003, Mr. H.O. Alamu 2003 – 2009, Rev. Mrs. B.A Ladoba 2009 – 2018 and Deacon Gbenga Abodunrin , became the principal in 2018

Some of the products of the school include: Sir Mobolaji Bank Anthony; Chief K. O. Mbadiwe; Sir Chief Kessington Adebutu Founder Premier Lotto (Baba Ijebu); Olu Oguntokun, former sports administrator and former Sole Administrator of Lagos State Sports Council; Ekundayo Opaleye Former military governor of Ondo State; Molade Okoya-Thomas; Olabisi Onabanjo, first civilian Governor of Ogun State, Babatunde Kwaku Adadevoh, Horatio Agedah Nigerian lawyer and journalist, Ahmed Yerima notable playwright, Senator Wahab Dosunmu; Ifagbemi Awamaridi, spiritualist, private detective; Senator Michael Opeyemi Bamidele; John Momoh CEO of Channels TV; Oba Funsho Adeolu, Prof Abisogun Leigh former vice chancellor of Lagos State University; Samuel Akintola, Femi Kuti musician; Ademola Adebise Managing Director/CEO Wema Bank PLC; Bade Aluko Chairman Great Nigeria Insurance Plc; Tayo Fatunla Cartoonist with BBC.

Sir Bank Anthony   Chief Olabisi Onabanjo   Chief K. O. Mbadiwe   Chief Kensington Adebutu

Chief Molade-Okoya   John Momoh   Femi Anikulapo-Kuti   Senator Opeyemi Bamidele

1.2.   CMS GRAMMAR SCHOOL, BARIGA LAGOS

CMS Grammar School is the oldest missionary secondary school and the first grammar school in Nigeria. The motto of the school is *Nisi Dominus Frustra*, which means without God, all is in vain (Psalm 127). The school was founded by the Church Missionary Society (CMS) in June 1859. The establishment of the school was anchored by Rev. Thomas Babington Macaulay and he was the first principal of the school. CMS is a Christian organization dedicated to the promotion of the Christian faith. With the approval letter of CMS, his stipend and the granted four rooms in a single storey building, the Cotton Warehouse, the old UTC Building on Broad Street, Lagos, Reverend Babington Macaulay started the school with 6 pupils. He trained as an Anglican Priest at the CMS Training

Institute Islington in the United Kingdom, where he studied Literary Arts, He was also a product of King's College, University of London where he obtained a Bachelor's degree in Arts. Thomas Babington Macaulay was ordained, next to The Rt. Revd Samuel Ajayi Crowther in 1854. Thomas Babington Macaulay was the father of Herbert Macaulay, one of the early nationalists in Nigerian politics. He served as the Principal of the school from 1859 to 1879 when he passed-on.

When CMS Grammar school was established, the primary schools in Lagos were not up to ten at the time. Expectedly, the school produced some of the first set of educated Nigerians and distinguished elites. Science subjects were introduced in 1915 and a science laboratory was built in 1929. The school moved in 1959, from Cotton House in Lagos-Island to its present location in Bariga. A large part of the school's land was lost in 1979 due to the government's policy to take-over all missionary schools. The history of the old school has been celebrated in a book published at its 150th anniversary.

The succeeding principals are: Archdeacon Henry Johnson succeeded Revd Macaulay in acting capacity in 1879 to 1881; Rt. Revd Isaac Oluwole, 1881 to 1893; Mr James Johnson 1893 to1894 (*acting*), Revd E. A. Godson, 1894 to 1895; Rt. Revd F. Melvile Jones, 1895-1896 (*acting*), The Revd Joseph Suberu Fanimokun, 1896 to 1914; Prof Canon E. J. Evans, 1915 to 1927; Revd A. Hobson, 1927 to 1929; Revd F. Watherton, 1929 to 1931, he was redeployed to establish Igbobi College; Venerable J. O. Lucas, 1932 to 1935 (*acting*); Revd C.G Thorne, 1935 to 1936; Rt. Revd S. O. Odutola, 1936 to 1938 (*acting*); Professor L. J. Lewis, 1938 to 1943; Rt. Revd Seth Irunsewe Kale, 1944 to 1949; Ven. B. A. Adelaja (an alumnus), 1950 to 1970; Mr. T. A. Ojo, 1970 to 1972 (*acting*); Sir High Chief Israel Akin Olowu, 1972 to 1984; Mr. B. A. Nigwo, (alumnus), 1985 to 1987; Mr. J. B. A. Edema, 1987 to 1997; Mr. Taiwo O. Jemilugba (alumnus), 1997 to 2001; Venerable J. O. Onayinka September 2001 to August 2005, and Venerable Tunde Oduwole (alumnus) September 2005 to 2017 and Venerable Adeyemi Ola Oluwa assumed duty as the principal in 2017. In 1919, Canon Evans composed the school song, which was later harmonized by Fela Sowande, an alumnus. The school was taken over by the government in 1979 and returned back to the mission in 2001. CMS Grammar School has produced quite a large number of distinguished Nigerians, some of them include: Messrs Herbert Macaulay, Akintola Williams, Prof Theophilus Ogunlesi, Chief Earnest Sonekan, Prof Ayodele Owolabi Major-General H.E.O. Adefope Otunba Niyi Adebayo, Tayo Shenbanjo, Dola Bamgboye, Dapo Adelegan and Femi Osanyinbi.

Herbert Macaulay   Akintola Williams   Prof Theophilus Ogunlesi   Chief Earnest Sonekan

Prof Ayodele Owolabi Major-General H.E O. Adefope Otunba Niyi Adebayo   Tayo Shenbanjo

22

Dola Bamgboye   Dapo Adelegan   Femi Osanyinbi

Gathering of Grammarians, some of the old students of the school

The old students constituted as the Grammarian Society of Nigeria in conjunction with Parents Teachers Association have invested in restoring the school back to the desired standard.

1.3. SAINT ANNE'S SCHOOL, IBADAN

St Anne's School, Ibadan had its origin in Kudeti Girls School that was founded in 1899 and CMS Girls School, Lagos, that was founded in 1869. The merger of the two schools in 1950 resulted to the name change to St Anne's School. Consequently, the institution can claim to be the oldest girls' secondary school in Nigeria. Mrs Abigail Macaulay, nee Ajayi Crowther and wife of the principal of CMS Grammar School was an advocate of the need for a secondary school for the girls. The school started with sixteen pupils and Mrs. Roper was the first principal. The name of the school was changed to CMS Girls Seminary in 1891 and in 1926, the name changed to CMS Girls School. Likewise, Kudeti Girls' School relocated to Molete in 1929 from Kudeti. The school chapel was commissioned in 1934 and it was named "Saint Anne's on the hill" and the ultimate name the school adopted till date. Considering the place of grandmothers in the upbringing up Yoruba children, Bishop Ajayi Crowther recommended the name of the mother of Mary, Saint Anne, the grandmother of Jesus, for the school. Also, the name of the wife of the pioneer missionary in Ibadan (1853-1869), David Hinderer was Anna.

Miss Wedmore and staff in 1959

Principals of the School over the years
Mrs Annie Roper 1869; Mrs Bonnetta Forbes Davies 1870 (acting), She was an adopted child of Queen Victoria; Rev Henry and Mrs Townsend were co-principals in 1871 to 1872; Rev and Mrs Mann, 1872 to 1885; Mrs Emma Harding née Kerr, 1885 to 1886; Mrs Vernall née Kruse, 1886 to 1888; Miss Marian Goodall, 1888 to 1893; Mrs Fanny Jones née Higgins (acting) 1894; Miss Ballson (acting), 1894 to 1905; Miss Boyton 1906; Miss Hill, 1906 to 1908; Mrs Wakeman, née Towe 1908; Miss Wait 1910 to 1927; Miss Mellor 1928 to 1931; Miss Grimwood 1931 to 1944; Miss Wedmore, 1944 to 1960; Mrs Bullock née Groves, 1960 to 1973; Mrs F. I. Ilori (acting), 1973; Mrs E. O. T. Makinwane, 1973 to 1984; Mrs Nike Ladipo 1984 to 1991; Mrs O. F. Osobamiro, 1991 to 1994; Mrs Dupe Babalola, 1995 to 2005; Mrs A. A. Kolapo, 2005 to 2007; Mrs F. I. Falomo, 2007 to 2014; Mrs K. A. Otesile 2014 to 2016; Mrs T. O. Orowale, 2016 to 2018; Mrs Y. O. Awe, 2018 to 2020.

1.4.   METHODIST BOYS HIGH SCHOOL, LAGOS

The African members of the Methodist Church of Nigeria established Wesleyan Boys' High School - Methodist Boys' High School (MBHS), Lagos. On the 14th of March in 1878, the school was formally commissioned by the colonial Governor, John D'Arcy Dumaresq. In April 1878, the first batch of students were admitted. George Stone Smith who later became known as Dr. Orishadipe Obasa of Ikija was among first twelve students to be were enrolled. The number of the enlisted students increased to twenty-three boys and seven agents by the end of the first year of establishing the school. The motto of the school from inception was *"Numquam non paratus"* (Never be unprepared). It was changed to *"Non sibi, sed aliis"* (Not for us, but for others) during the tenure of Mr Euba who became the school principal in 1889. Methodist Boys' High School started on Broad Street, Lagos and retained the site until relocation to 5.7-acre parcel of land in Victoria Island, Lagos after over 100 years. The new site was allocated to the school in 1983, a compensation for the initially allocated 60-hectare of land in Ojoo, Badagry that was taken over by the Lagos State Government for the use of the Lagos State University. The school houses are Didsbury House, Handsworth House, Kingswood House and Westminster House. The school operates on the Victoria Island site.

School Principals of MBHS Over the Years
Rev. W. Terry Coppin was the first principal and was ably assisted by W. B. Euba and J. H. Samuel. The successive school principals are: Rev. W. Terry Coppin, 1878–1883; Rev. George W. Baxter, 1883–1884; Rev Edmund Tomlin, 1884; Rev. M. J. Elliott, 1885; Rev. J. H. Wellington, 1886–1889; Rev. W. B. Euba, 1889–1896; Rev. J. H. Samuel, 1896–1902; Rev. W. B. Euba, 1902–1912; Rev. A. W. Moulton Wood, 1912–1918; Rev. H. W. Stacey, 1919–1927; Rev. J. A. Angus, 1927–1932; Mr. J. T. Jackson, 1932–1943; Rev. W. Roberts, 1943–1946; Mr. A. B. Oyediran (Old Boy), 1947–1955; Rev. S. A. Osinulu, 1956–1962; Chief. D. A. Famoroti, 1962–1979; Mr. O. O. Soewu (the first alumnus to be the principal of the school), 1979–1981 and 2004–2005; Chief. A. A. Osuneye (alumnus), 1981-1989; Mr. E. F. Olukunle (alumnus), 1990–1994; Prince. S. O. Saibu, 1995–2001; Mr. Ademola Johnson (alumnus), 2001–2004; Rev. S. A. Ogunniyi, 2005–2007; Mr. J. A. Oyegbile (acting), 2007–2008; The Rev Samuel O. Osinubi, 2008–2009; Mr. F. F. Akinsete (acting), 2009; The Rev. Titus Kayode Fatunla, 2009–2012; The Very Rev Capt. Phillip

Okunoren (alumnus), 2012–October 2015; The Very Rev. David Oyebade, October 2015–October 2016 and The Very Rev Paul Olukunga assumed duty in October 2016.

Some of the Prominent Alumni of MBHS

Dr. Nnamdi Azikiwe   Chief Olusegun Osoba Senator Adolphus Wabara   Chief Rasheed Gbadamosi

Like the other heritage schools, MBHS has produced so many distinguished Nigerians. Some of the products of the school include: Dr. Nnamdi Azikiwe Chief Segun Osoba Senator Adolphus Wabara, Chief Rasheed Gbadamosi, Prof. H.O.I. Thomas, VC UI, Prof. Oladele Ajose 1st VC University of Ife, Justice G.B. Coker, Chief Justice Fatai Williams, Justice Y.A. Jinadu, Admiral Adekunle Lawal, Brigadier General Mobolaji Johnson, Air Marshal Nureni Yusuf, Vice Admiral Babatunde Elegbede, Mr. Fola Adeola, Dele Adelodun, Pastor (Dr.) D.K. Olukoya HRM Oba

Justice Fatai Williams   Oba Funso Adeolu   Brig-Gen Mobolaji Johnson Oba M.A. Sonariwo

| Dele Adelodun | Fola Adeola | Pastor D.K. Olukoya | Oba Saheed Elegushi |

1.5. METHODIST GIRLS' HIGH SCHOOL, YABA, LAGOS

Methodist Girls' High School (MGHS), Yaba in Lagos-State (formerly Wesleyan Girls' High School), was established in 1879. It is a sister school of Methodist Boys High School in Lagos and the second female secondary school and the fourth oldest secondary school in Nigeria., this is the sister school to Methodist Boys High School and is the third oldest secondary school in Nigeria after CMS Grammar School and Methodist Boys High School Miss Sarah Elizabeth Smith was the first principal of the school. Mrs Charlotte Olajumoke Obasa and Mrs Victoria Onafowokan also served as the principal of the school for many years. Some of the prominent alumni of MGHS include Chief (Mrs) H.I.D. Awolowo, Professor Ibiyinka Fuwape, Alhaja Lateefat Okunnu and Chief (Mrs) Folake Solanke SAN, Mrs Ibukun Awosika, Erelu Bisi Fayemi.

Chief H.I.D. Awolowo   Mrs Folake Solanke   Mrs Ibukun Awosika   Erelu Bisi Fayemi

1.6. HOPE WADDEL TRAINING INSTITUTE, CALABAR

One of the earliest secondary school founded in the semblance of an industrial centre, was the Hope Waddell Training Institute in Calabar, Cross River State of Nigeria. It was established in 1895 by the missionaries of the United Presbyterian Church of Scotland.

Mary Mitchell Slessor, a Scottish missionary who got to Calabar in 1876 was a notable driving force behind the establishment of the school which started in 1895. The school was named after Reverend Hope Masterton Waddel. 42 students were in the school in 1900 and vocation thought included gardening, printing, tailoring, engineering, carpentry and baking. The successive principals of the school include: W.R. Thompson, a Scottish 1895 to 1902; James Luke, a Scottish 1902 to 1907; J. K. Macgregor, a Scottish 1907 to 1943; E. B. Jones, a Scottish 1943 to 45; N. C. Macrae, a Scottish 1945 to 1952; J. A. T. Beattie, a Scottish 1952 to 1957; Sir Dr. Francis Akanu Ibiam, an Igbo 1957 to 1960; B. E. Okon, an Efik 1960 to 1974.

Mary Mitchell Slessor

Some of the notable products of the institute included: Prof Eni Njoku, Prof John Ogbu, Kingsley O. Mbadiwe, Dennis Osadebay, Akanu Ibiam, Alex Mascot Ikwechegh, Prof Anya Oko Anya, Eyo Ita, Dr. Nnamdi Azikiwe, Eze Cyril Akagbulem Unamka, Vice Admiral Edet Akinwale Wey and Senator Joseph Oqua Ansa.

Akanu Ibiam   Prof Eni Njoku   Chief D. Osadebay V/A Akin Wey   Prof Anya Oko   Anya Eyo Ita

CHAPTER TWO

THE FIRST TWO DECADES IN THE 20TH CENTURY: 1900-1920

2.1. METHODIST BOY'S HIGH SCHOOL, ORON

Methodist Boys' High School (MBHS), Oron was initially named Oron Training Institute. It later transformed from teacher's training school to primary school, high school, and a comprehensive high school. MBHS Oron was established on the 18th of September in 1905 in order to provide sound academic ground for the bright schoolboys. The influence of Rev. Nathaniel Boocock on the founding of the school must be acknowledged; he was a primeval Methodist Church priest who had remarkable pioneering efforts in the west coast of Africa, that led to creation of missions. The ethos of the school was that of an English public school with focus on character training while giving priority to Christian religion. Right from the time the school was established. Akwa Ibom-State government returned the school to the original owner, Methodist Mission in 2006.

Past School Principals: The successive school principals over the years are: Rev. W. J. Ward, 1905 to 1907; Rev. T. W. Hancox, 1907 to 1911; Rev. C. P. Groves, 1912 to 1924; Rev. C. W. Showell, 1924 to 1926; Mr. W. T. Smith, 1927 to 1929; Rev. E. E. Pritchard,1929 to 1931; Rev. C. E. Wiles, 1932 to 1938; Rev. N. E. Boulton, 1938 to 1945; Rev. C. E. Wiles, 1945 to 1955; Rev. S. K. Okpo, 1956 to 1961; Mr. W. W. Anderson, 1961 to 1964; Mr. C. N. Iroanya, 1964 to 1965; Mr. E. E. Bassey, 1965 to 1970; Mr. O. W. Inyang, 1970 to 1971; Mr. A. U. Umo, 1971 to 1973; Mr. U. S. Ekpo, 1973 to 1974; Messrs P. O. Akpan & M. A. Eyo, 1975 to 1976; Mr. U. S. Ekpo, 1976 to 1978; Chief O. O. Awatt, 1978 to 1980; Mr R. A. Ekanem, 1980 to 1983; Mr A. E. Udofia, 1983 to 1984; Mr. E. O. Akaiso, 1984 (9 months); Mr. O. U. Bassey, 1984 to 1985; Chief A. A. Ntuen, 1985 to 1988; Mr. A. E. Onwineng, 1988 (2 months); Mr. E. E. Essien, 1988 to 1989; Mr. E. O. Uwe, 1989 to 1990; Mr. O. U. Ide, 1990 to 1993; Elder S. T. Uko, 1993 to 1995; Mr. E. Okwong-Udo, 1995 to 1998, Mr. Ukpe Unanaowo, 1998–2000; Mr. Effiong A. Afahakan, 2000 to 2001; Mrs. Ubong E. Bassey,2001 to 2006; Chief O. U. Bassey, 2006 to 2007; Rev. Ini Atti, 2008 to 2010, Elder E. B. Esu, 2010 to 2011; Mr. Effiong Jonah Mfon, 2011 to 2012; Mrs. Ubong Bassey, 2012 to 2017; Mrs. Aniema Bassey, 2017 to 2018 and Mrs. Nene B. Esin, became principal in 2018.

2.2. ABEOKUTA GRAMMAR SCHOOL

The Abeokuta District Anglican Church Council, founded Abeokuta Grammar School (AGS) in 1908. The students of the school were enrolled for examination by the Royal College of Preceptors in 1909 and sat for the Cambridge Local Examination in 1911. In 1914, it became a mixed school of males and females with the admission of girls. The school presented students for the Cambridge School Certificate Examination in 1939. AGS was elevated to the status of a model-school by the Nigerian government in 1996. Some of the products of the school include: Prof Wole Soyinka Dr Beko Ransome-Kuti, Fela Anikulapo Kuti, Oba Okunade Sijuade, Tunde Kelani, and Mrs Funmilayo Ransome-Kuti

Mrs Funmi Ransome-Kuti Dr. B. A. Onafowokan   Prof Wole Soyinka   Dr Beko Ransome-Kuti

Oba Okunade Sijuade   Fela Anikulapo Kuti   Tunde Kelani

2.3. KINGS COLLEGE, LAGOS

The number one among the very prestigious secondary schools founded by the colonial government in Nigeria is the King's College, Lagos. The boys' school only was established by an Act of British Parliament, on Monday 20th of September in 1909 as boys only school. The recommendation of Henry Rawlingson Carr, who was the Nigerian Acting Director of Education in Lagos to Governor Walter Egerton in 1908 formed the basis of establishing the school by the colonial government. The mission of the founding fathers was "to provide for the youth of the colony a higher general education than that supplied by the existing Schools, to prepare them for Matriculation Examination of the University of London and to give a useful course of Study to those who intend to qualify for professional life or to enter government or mercantile service." The King's School, Lagos as it was initially called started with ten students. Messrs J. C. Vaughan, Isaac Ladipo Oluwole (the first senior prefect), Frank Macaulay, Herbert Mills (from Ghana), O. A. Omololu and Moses King were among the pioneer students. The pioneer teaching staff consisted of three Europeans and two African assistant teachers. Number of registered students was 16 at the end of 1910 and it rose to 67 in December 1914.

The first headmaster of the college was Sir Lomax who was succeeded by G.H. Hyde-Johnson in 1910; while McKee Wright was in charge till 1917. Other school principals were Messrs J. A. de Gaye, 1917 to 1919; D. L. Kerr 1919; H. A. A. F. Harman, 1919 to

1925; W. M. Peacock, 1926 to 1931; J. N. Panes 1931 to 1936; A. H Clift 1936 to 1947; A. D. Porter 1947; G. P. Savage 1948; J. R. Bunting, 1949 to 1954; P. H. Davis, 1957 to 1964; Rex Akpofure, 1964 to 1968, the first indigenous principal; R. S. G. Agiobu-Kemmer, 1968 to1975; M. O. Imana, 1975 to 1978; Augustine A. Ibegbulam, 1978 to 1985; S. O. Agun, 1985 to 1992 and S. A. Akinruli 1992 to 1994. S. I. Balogun, Sylvester Onoja, Yetunde Awofuwa – the first female principal of the school, Akintoye A. Ojemuyiwa and Otunba Oladele Olapeju were also the succeeding principal.

Some of the Prominent Old Students of King's College

Like other great schools in Nigeria, King's College has produced many distinguished Nigerians that include Chief Simeon Adebo, Justice Adetokunbo Ademola, Oba Adeyinka Oyekan, Chief Anthony Enahoro, Dr Samuel Manuwa, Fela Sowande, Lateef Jakande, Alex Ekwueme, Alhaji Lateef Adegbite, Victor Ovie Whisky, Claude Ake, Sam Akpabot, Ephraim Akpata, Chief Emeka Ojukwu, Brigadier-General Christopher Oluwole Rotimi, Lateef Olufemi Okunnu, Audu Ogbeh, Rotimi Alakija, Atedo Peterside, Wale Adenuga, Sola Akinyede, Cobhams Asuquo, Bayo Ogunlesi, Hakeem Bello-Osagie, Russel Dikko, Arnold Ekpe , Ibrahim Gambari, Akanu Ibiam, Asue Ighodalo, Pastor Ituah Ighodalo, Oladipo Jadesimi, Adetokunbo Lucas, Vincent I. Maduka, Audu Maikori, Babagana Monguno, Gogo Chu Nzeribe, Adebayo Ogunlesi, Kole Omotosho, Sanusi Lamido Sanusi, Senator Bukola Saraki, Fola Osekita, Kayode Oyawoye, Senator Udoma Udo Udoma, Shamsudeen Usman, James Churchill Vaughan, Edikan Ekong.

Chief Simeon Adebo   Sir Adetokunbo Ademola Oba Adeyinka Oyekan   Chief Anthony Enahoro

Alhaji Lateef Jakande   Dr Alex Ekwueme   Emeka Odumegwu-Ojukwu   Ephraim Akpata

Claude Ake   Audu Ogbeh   Shamsudeen Usman   Hakeem Bello-Osagie

Atedo Peterside   Pastor Ituah Ighodalo   Alhaji Sanusi Lamido   Senator Bukola Saraki

2.4. IJEBU-ODE GRAMMAR SCHOOL

Ijebu-Ode Grammar School was established as co-educational school in 1913. The school is considered as the oldest in Ijebu land and the second oldest secondary school in Ogun-State. The school started in a private residential property before relocating to the vicarage of St. Saviour's Church in Ijasi, where it remained until the permanent location in Ijebu-Ode, on Abeokuta Road. The school houses are: Kuti House, Johnson House, Odumosu House, Gansallo House, Phillips House. Some of the prominent products of the school include Senator Abraham Adesanya, Nigerian lawyer and political activist; Chief Adeola Odutola, Nigerian business mogul; Justice Inumidun Akande, former Chief Judge of Lagos State; Sir Mobolaji Bank Anthony, former council President of the Lagos Stock Exchange; George Ashiru, Taekwondo grandmaster; Harold Demuren, Nigerian aeronautic engineer; Chief Bode George, Nigerian Politician and former Military Governor of Ondo-State; Rt. Rev. Seth Kale, former Bishop of Lagos; Senator Adeleke Mamora, onetime Minister of State for Health and Senator Omololu Meroyi.

Chief Adeola Odutola   Senator Abraham Adesanya Chief Bode George   Senator Ade Mamora

Sir Bank Anthony

2.5.   EKO BOYS HIGH SCHOOL, MUSHIN, LAGOS 1913

Eko Boys' High School was founded on 13th of January in 1913 by Reverend William Benjamin Euba, a Methodist priest. His desire was to establish a secondary school that would provide educational opportunities for the less privileged citizens of Lagos. Amongst the Old boys of the school are: Brigadier Ola Oni, Dr Abubakar Olusola Saraki, Major General Adeyinka Adebayo, Chief Gabriel Igbinedion, Babatunde Fashola SAN, Akiogun of Iru Land, Oba Idowu Abiodun Oniru; Onilogbo of Ilogbo, Oba Ayinde Olaleye; Chief Segun Olushola, Chief Idowu Sofola (SAN), Justice Muri Okunola and Alao Aka-Bashorun.

Chief Gabriel Igbinedion   Maj-Gen. R. A. Adebayo   Senator Olusola Saraki   Justice Idowu Sofola

Chief Segun Olushola   Alao Aka-Bashorun SAN   Babatunde Fashola SAN

2.6. IBADAN GRAMMAR SCHOOL

Ibadan Grammar School (IGS) was established on the 31st of March in 1913 as a Christian school, by Rt Rev Alexander Babatunde Akinyele an Anglican priest. It was males only in the first 31 years of its establishment and became co-educational in 1941. The 1st principal was Bishop Akinyele who was succeeded by Rev E. L. Latunde 1933-1948, Rev E. A. Odusanwo 1940-1948 and Venerable Emmanuel O. Alayande the legendary principal from 1948 to 1968. The IGS moved to the 58-acre permanent site on March 5, 1951 In the 1950s and 1960s, the Higher School Certificate was included in the school system.. Some of the prominent old students include Mike Adénúgà, Chief Ayọ̀ Rosiji, Chief Oladitan, Prof Michael Ọmọlẹwà, Abdul Hamid Adiamoh, Alex Ibru, Olúṣẹgun Àgàgú, Chief Bọ́lá Ìgè and Michael Ọlátúnjí Ọnàjídé.

Prof Akin Mabogunje

Chief Oladitan

Chief Bola Ige

Alex Ibru

Prof Michael Omolewa

Dr. Segun Agagu

Michael Adenuga

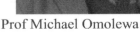

2.7.   ETINAN INSTITUTE, ETINAN, AKWA-IBOM 1915

Etinan institute was established in 1915 by Qua Iboe Mission and Mr R. J. Taylor was the first principal. Mr Emeti E. Anana is the 28th principal of the institution as at the time of publishing the first edition of this book, when the school had 47 teaching and 15 non-teaching staff with the students' population of 3,427 in 68 streams (sections). The school is coeducational and has boarding facilities with over 500 students in the ratio of 50:50 male to female students. The old students of the institution include 3 ex-state governors, a secretary to the Federal Government of Nigeria, a secretary to the state government, a university vice-chancellor, commissioners, permanent secretaries among other dignitaries.

2.8.   ONDO BOYS HIGH SCHOOL

Ondo Boys' High School (OBHS) was founded by the Ondo community on the 13th of January 1919. The school motto is *Probitas Nationem Extolit* (righteousness exalteth a nation) and the school song is "There is beauty all around". The founding principal was Canon Moses Craig Akinpelumi Adeyemi, a classics scholar who attended St Andrew's College, Oyo to train as a teacher and later graduated from FourFadah Bay College. Other succeeding principals include Messrs Akinrele, Awosika, Akintemi, Iluyomade and Canon Ariyo. Prominent old students, Archdeacon Jonathan Abiodun Iluyomade, Chief D.O. Adetunmbi (father of the author and the Attah of Egbira land, King Ado Ibrahim.

Chief D.O. Adetunmbi   Ven. J. A. Iluyomade   Alhaji Ado Ibrahim

The school Prefects of Ondo Boys High School in 1944 in Ondo-State of Nigeria. Sitting L-R: C. Afolabi, Archdeacon J. A. Iluyomade, the Principal, J. Olarinde and Chief David Opeyemi Adetunmbi. Standing L-R: R. S. Rogers, D. Olomukoro, D. Atteka, B. Ogunti, Bakare and Ajalosi.

CHAPTER THREE

SCHOOLS FOUNDED BETWEEN 1920 AND 1930

3.1.   BAREWA COLLEGE, ZARIA

Barewa College was founded in 1927 by British Governor General Hugh Clifford, in Zaria, Kaduna State in the northern part of Nigeria. The school was originally named as Katsina College. The name changed to Kaduna College in 1938 and to Government College, Zaria in 1949 and finally settled for Barewa College. It is a notable boarding school located in Tudun Wadda area pf the city. The dormitories in the college are namely: Bello Kagara House, Lugard House, Clifford House, Dan Hausa House, Mallam Smith House, Nagwamatse House, Bienemann House, Mort House, Jafaru House and Suleiman Barau House. It is also the most-celebrated post-primary school reputed for having a large number of prominent elites from the northern region as products. Among its remarkable alumni were Tafawa Balewa who was Prime Minister of Nigeria from 1960 to 1966 and four former military Heads of State of Nigeria. Notable alumni of Barewa include: Ahmadu Bello, 1st Premier of Northern Nigeria; Abubakar Tafawa Balewa, Prime Minister of Nigeria; Hassan Katsina, Governor of Northern Nigeria; Yakubu Gowon , Nigerian military Head of State (HoS); Murtala Mohammed, military HoS; Shehu Shagari, President of Nigeria; Umaru Musa Yar'Adua, President of Nigeria; Ibrahim Dasuki, Sultan of Sokoto; Sa'adu

Abubakar, Sultan of Sokoto; Shehu Abubakar, Emir of Gombe (1984-2014); Mohammed Bello, Chief Justice of Nigeria; Abdulkadir Ahmed, Governor of CBN; Ibrahim Mahmud Alfa, military Governor of Kaduna State; Prof Jubril Aminu, former Ambassador to the USA; Adamu Ciroma, Governor of CBN; Ibrahim Coomassie, Inspector General of the Nigerian Police; Umaru Dikko, Minister for Transportation; Nasir Ahmad el-Rufai, Governor of Kaduna State and Mallam Isiaka Abdulrazaq.

Alhaji Ahmadu Bello   Alhaji Tafawa Balewa   Alhaji Shehu Shagari   General Yakubu Gowon

General M. Mohammed   Shehu Musa Yar'Adua   Sultan Ibrahim Dasuki   Dr Adamu Ciroma

Prof Jubril Aminu   Sultan Saad Abubakar   Nasir El-Rufai   Isiaka Abdulrazaq

3.2. QUEEN'S COLLEGE, LAGOS

The Queen's College (QC) in Yaba, Lagos is a federal government-owned girl's secondary that was founded in 1927 when Nigeria was still a British colony. It has boarding facilities and often referred to as the "sister college" of the King's College, Lagos. The school is reputed for having the best results nationwide in the West African Senior School Certificate Examination conducted by the West African Examinations Council since 1985 for over seven times. Expectedly, QC is widely considered to be one of the top female schools in Nigeria and its environs. "Pass on the Torch" is the motto of Queen's College. The school remains committed to bringing out the best in girls and girl child education. The vision to produce generations of women who will excel, compete globally and contribute meaningfully to nation building is sustained.

The succeeding school principals over the years were Miss F. Wordsworth (later Mrs. Tolfree), 1927 to 1930; Miss W. W. Blackwell, 1931 to 1942; Mrs. D. Mather, 1942 to 1944; Dr. Alice Whittaker, 1944 to 1946; Miss Ethel Hobson, 1946 to 1950; Miss Mary Hutcheson,1950 to 1954; Miss Joyce Moxon, 1954 to 1955; Miss Margaret. Gentle (later Mrs. Harwood), 1956 to 1963; Mrs. I. E. Coker, 1963 to 1977 (First Nigerian principal of Queen's college); Mrs. T. E. Chukwuma, 1978 to 1982; Mrs. A. A Kafaru, 1982 to 1986; Mrs. J. E. Ejueyitche, 1986 to 1987; Mrs. J. Namme, 1987 to 1991; Mrs. H. E. G. Marinho, 1991 to 1996; Mrs. M. T.F. Sojinrin, 1996 to 2001; Mrs. O. O. Euler-Ajayi, 2001 to 2004; Mrs. M. B. Abolade, 2004 to 2006; Mrs. O. Togonu-Bickersteth, 2006 to 2008; Mrs. A. C. Onimole, 2008 to 2010; Mrs. A. Ogunnaike, 2010 to 2011; Mrs. M. O. A. Ladipo, 2011 to 2012; Mrs E. M. Osime, 2012 to 2015; Dr Mrs Lami Amodu, 2015 to 2017; Mrs B. A. Are, 2017 to 2018 and Dr Mrs Oyinloye Yakubu who assumed duty in 2018.

Prominent alumni members include Suzanne Iroche, Claire Ighodaro, née Ukpoma, Phebean Ogundipe née Itayemi, Modupe Omo-Eboh (the first female judge in Nigeria),

Sefi Atta, Lara George, Honey Ogundeyi, Grace Alele-Williams (the first female vice chancellor of a Nigerian university) and Prof. Folashade Ogunsola

Sherman Rosenberg of Chicago, a chemistry teacher Phoebean Ogundipe was playing basketball with QC students

Prof Grace Alele-Williams

Prof Folasade Ogunsola   Mrs Ibirobo Adekola   Mrs Labake Adetunmbi   Mrs Taiwo Adejumo

3.3.   GOVERNMENT COLLEGE, IBADAN

Government College Ibadan (GCI) was founded by the colonial government in 1927. The founding fathers of the college were Messrs Selwyn MacGregor Grier, Director of Education, Southern Provinces, who conceived the idea of the school and E. R. Swanston, Inspector of Education. The school was formally established on the 28th of February in 1929 with the first set of 29 students. The first principal was C. E. Squire who succeeded by H.

T. C. Field while V. B. V. Powell was the third principal. GCI was modelled after a typical the British public boarding school of the era. During the Second World War, the school temporarily moved to several sites before finally resettling back at its original site. The school houses are Carr House (Orange), Field House (Green), Grier House (Maroon), Powell House (Purple) and Swanston House (Blue).

Among the prominent old students were Adegoke Adelabu, Akinola Aguda, the first Chief Justice of Botswana, T. M. Aluko, Segun Awolowo, Wale Babalakin, Cyprian Ekwensi, King Erediauwa, Abel Guobadia, Christopher Kolade, Ifedayo Oladapo, Victor Omololu Olunloyo ,Femi Osofisan, Ayo Rosiji, Ven P. B. Oyebolu, Prof Wole Soyinka. In March 2022, the Oyo State Government signed handover agreement of the College to the Government College Ibadan Old Boys Association (GCIOBA) for management, operation, and development. This was in response to the request of GCIOBA to manage, operate and develop the school in order to maintain and sustain its legacy and the preeminent status of the institution. The incorporated Board of Trustees made up of the nominees of the state government, GCIOBA and the parents association was granted "the right and authority to take charge. The new management will be responsible for the provision of additional infrastructure and improvement of existing ones in the school among other responsibilities.

Ven P. B. Oyebolu   Prof Wole Soyinka   Dr Chris Kolade   Oba Erediauwa

Adegoke Adelabu   Justice Akinola Aguda   Dr Victor Olunloyo   Cyprian Ekwensi

Wale Babalakin SAN   Sina Fagbenro-Byron   Bolade Oyebolu   Abi Adigun

44

3.4. GOVERNMENT COLLEGE, UMUAHIA, ABIA

Government College Umuahia (GCU) is a secondary school for boys that was established by the British colonial government in 1927, about 2 decades after the King's College in Lagos was established. It was the same year that similar public schools for males were founded - Government College, Ibadan and Government College Zaria (now Barewa College). Like KC, the schools were planned to follow the traditions of the standard British public schools such as Eton, Harrow and Winchester. GCU is located on Umuahia-Ikot Ekpene road in Umuahia and was known as the 'Eton of the East,' at that time because it was located in Nigeria's orient and reputed for its high standards in all fronts. The founding school Principal was Rev. Robert Fisher, an English educator, a mathematician and an Anglican priest. He got to Umuahia in 1927 and acquired 26 km square land. On January 29, 1929 he formally started the school with 25 students drawn from all parts of Nigeria and West Africa, yet with catchment in the Eastern Nigeria and the Southern Cameroons. The school started as a teacher training institute and in 1930, it converted to a secondary school. Fisher was in charge until 1939 when he left for England at the start of the Second World War. He was succeeded by W. N. Tolfree. The school was closed for three years while the students and staff were relocated to King's College, Lagos and to other mission schools east of the Niger and the school premises was used as a Prisoner of War camp for the detaining of German and Italian prisoners captured in Cameroon by the British.

The Government College Umuahia Old Boys Association set up Fisher Educational Trust and on December 22, 2014, the Deed of Trust was signed with the Abia State government, thereby vesting the Trust with all legal interests, rights and power pertaining to ownership, management, operation, control and funding of Government College Umuahia.

Some of the prominent old students include Messrs Ben Enwonwu, Jaja Wachukwu,

The first Speaker of the House of Representatives and Nigeria's first foreign minister, Arikpo Okoi, E. M. L. Endeley, a former premier of Southern Cameroon, Victor Mukete, Nigeria's first minister of information, Kelsey Harrison, Nelson Enwerem, Chinua Achebe, Elechi Amadi, George Kurubo, the first Nigerian Chief of the Nigerian Air Force, Gabriel Okara, Chukwuemeka Ike, Ken Saro-Wiwa, Nimi Briggs, I. N. C. Aniebo, Christopher Okigbo, Dick W. Emuchay, Okechukwu Nwadiuto Emuchay, Kelechi Amadi-Obi, Uche James-Iroha, Jide Obi, Lazarus Ekwueme, Akpabio, J.O.J. Okezie, Nigeria's first minister of health, Chu Okongwu, Edmund Daukoru, Mofia Tonjo Akobo, Nigeria's first minister of petroleum, Peter Katjavivi, Okechukwu Enelamah, Obi Nwakanma, Chukwuedu Nwokolo, Domingo Okorie, Achike Udenwa, Orji Uzor Kalu, Okwesilieze Nwodo, Charles Onyeama, Anthony Aniagolu, and Idah Peterside.

Chinua Achebe   Ben Enwonwu   Jaja Wachukwu   Arikpo Okoi

Christopher Okigbo   Prof Lazarus Ekwueme   Ken Saro-Wiwa   Orji Uzor Kalu

3.5.   ST. GREGORY COLLEGE, IKOYI, LAGOS

St Gregory College located Ikoyi, Lagos was established by the Catholic mission in 1928 and named after Pope St. Gregory the Great (540–604). The college, was initially a mixed (male and female) campus until the creation of its sister school, Holy Child College Obalende, in the South West of Ikoyi. St. Gregory's College that was founded on 27th of January in 1928 is the oldest of all the schools in the Archdiocese of Lagos. The motto of the school is *Pro Fide et Scientia* (For faith and knowledge). The early pioneering effort of establishing the school was attributed to Right Reverend Ferdinand Terrien for the purpose of giving young boys a holistic education that is built on the pillars of the fear of God and sound knowledge of all there is to know. The past principals of the school were: Archbishop Leo Hale Taylor, 1928-1934; Rev. Fr. James Saul, 1934-1937; Rev. Fr. Francis Bunyan, 1938-1942, Rev. Fr. T.J. Moran, 1943-1957; Rev. Fr. T.J. MacAndrew, 1957-1959; Rev. Fr. James MacCarthy, 1960-1969; Rev. Fr. Francis McGovern, 1969-1972; Mr. Paul Amenechi, 1972-1977; Mr. Anthony Omoera, 1977-1992; Mr. Anthony Bolawa, 1992-1993; Mr. C.B. Adekoya, 1994-1999; Mr. M.A. Salami, 2000-2001; Monsignor Edmund Akpala, 2001-2014 and Rev. Fr Emmanuel Ayeni took charge in 2015. As at the point of publishing this book, the Most Rev. Alfred Adewale Martin was the Metropolitan Archbishop of Lagos and the College Proprietor. Prominent old students include Justice Adetokunbo Ademola, Sir Adeyemo Alakija KBE, Cardinal Anthony Olubunmi Okogie, Victor Uwaifo, Funsho Williams, Oba Lamidi Adeyemi III, Alaafin of Oyo, Chief Ayo G. Irikefe, Sir Lambert Akinyede, Ade A. Olufeko, Ganiyu Dawodu, Oba C. D. Akran, A. Deinde Fernandez, Jab Adu, Jimi Agbaje, Ben Murray Bruce, Adewale Maja-Pearce, J. M. Johnson, Jibril Martin, Bode Rhodes-Vivour, Raymond Njoku, Olufemi Majekodunmi, Patrick Ekeji, Tayo Aderinokun, Obafemi Lasode, Segun Agbaje and Denrele Edun.

Adeyemo Alakija   Justice A. Ademola Ayo G. Irokefe   Cardinal Olubunmi Okogie

Sir Lambert Akinyede   Oba Lamidi Adeyemi   Dehinde Fanadez   Raymond Njoku

Funso Williams   Jab Adu   Victor Uwaifo   Ben Murray-Bruce

Tayo Aderinnokun   Jimi Agbaje   Ayo George   Patrick Oke

48

CHAPTER FOUR

THE SCHOOLS ESTABLISHED IN 1931 TO 1940

4.1. IGBOBI COLLEGE, LAGOS

Igbobi College (IC) was jointly established in 1932 by the Wesleyan Methodist Mission and Church Missionary Society (Anglican Communion). founding of Igbobi College was a follow-up to the 1926 Education Code, which was itself an attempt to revise and improve upon Lugard's Education Code of 1916. The school is situated in the Yaba suburb of Lagos. Lagos state government took-over the ownership of the school in 1979 and in 2001, it was returned to its original owners by the state government. Some of the prominent old students of the include Justice Taslim Olawale Elias, Prof J. F. Ade Ajayi, Chief Olu Falae, Chief Michael Ibru, Chief K. O. Mbadiwe, Chief Subomi Balogun, Chief Chris Ogunbanjo, Vice Admiral Akintunde Aduwo, Prof Segun Fayemi, Segun Awolowo, Felix Ibru, Yemi Osinbajo, Babatunde Fashola, Bolaji Akinyemi, Femi Kuti, Gbolahan Mudasiru, Ernest Shonekan, Lanre Tejuosho, Babatunde Fowler, Femi Gbajabiamila, Prof Gbolahan Elias, Paul Adefarasin Sola Adebayo, Yinka Oladitan, Dele Balogun.

Justice Teslim Elias Chief Chris Ogunbanjo Prof J. Ade Ajayi Chief M. Ibru Chief Olu Falae

49

Chief Subomi Balogun   V. Admiral Akin Aduwo   Prof Bolaji Akinyemi Prof Segun Fayemi

Segun Awolowo   Chief Felix Ibru   Prof Yemi Osinbajo   Pastor Paul Adefarasin

Prof Gbolahan Elias Hon Femi Gbajabiamila   Babatunde Fashola   Niyi Emiabata

4.2.   CHRIST THE KING COLLEGE, ONITSHA

Christ the King College (CKC), Onitsha is a secondary school for males. It was founded on February 2, 1933 by Archbishop Charles Heerey and his fellow Irish missionaries. The most reverend Heerey remained the proprietor of the school until his death in the spring of 1967. CKC has been ranked very high in standard over the years. According to a published report, it was ranked the number 1 high school in Nigeria and the 36th in the top 100 best high schools in Africa in February 2014. The first principal of the college was Rev Fr. Leo Brolly and the first student to be admitted into the college was Peter Charles Obi Nwagbogu. The pre-civil war School Houses were St. Charles, St. Gabriel, St Williams, St Michael's and St. Joseph. All the school houses are now named after Tagbo, Brolly, Azikiwe, Heerey, Okagbue, Modebe, Arinze, Aniogu, Mbanefo, Orjiakor, Allagoa, Butler, and Flanagan.

The succeeding school principals were Rev Fr. W.L. Brolly 1933–1937, Rev. Fr. M Flanagan 1938–1941, Rev. Fr J. Keane 1942–1943, Rev. Fr. A. Callaghan 1943, Rev. Fr. M. Flanagan 1943–1948, Rev. Fr. M. Clifford 1949–1953, Rev. Fr. W Butler 1953–1954, Rev. Fr. J. Keane 1955–1956, Rev. Fr. J. Fitz Patrick 1956–1963, Rev. Fr. N. C. Tagbo 1963–1972 (First indigenous principal), Chief A.A.O. Ezenwa 1973–1974, Rev. H. Chiwuzie 1974–1975, Mr. P. E. Ezeokeke 1975–1976, Rev. Fr. N. C. Tagbo 1976–1985, Mr. M. N. Enemou 1985–1987, Rev. Dr. V. A. Nwosu 1987–1996, Mr. J. E. Chukwurah 1996–1997, Mr. E. C. Umeh 1997–2000, Chief N. E. Olisah 2000–2008, Chief A. Obika: 2008–2009, Mr. E. Ezenduka 2009–2010, Rev. Fr. Charles Okwumuo 2010–2019 and the 23rd principal is Rev. Fr. Dr. Celestine Arinze Okafor, he came on board in 2019.

Prominent among the old students include Ezeolisa Allagoa, Dr. Pius N.C. Okigbo, Justice Chukwudifu Akunne Oputa, Arc. Frank Nwobuora Mbanefo, Dr. Peter Odili, Prof. Patrick Utomi, Olisa Agbakoba SAN, Justice Anthony Aniagolu, Justice Chukwunweike Idigbe, Chike Francis Ofodile, Peter Obi, Willie Obiano, Archbishop Valerian M. Okeke, Mr Oseloka H. Obaze, Justice Peter N. C Umeadi and John Munonye.

51

Justice C. A. Oputa   Ezeolisa Allagoa   Dr Pius Okigbo   Arch. F. N. Mbanefo

Justice A. Aniagolu   Dr Peter Odili   Olisa Agbakoba SAN   Prof Patrick Utomi

Peter Obi   Willie Obiano   Justice Peter Umeadi Archbishop V. Okeke

4.3.   CHRIST'S SCHOOL, ADO-EKITI

Christ's School, Ado-Ekiti was founded by a British Priest, Venerable Henry Dallimore. The institution started as Ekiti Central School in 1933 and admitted pupils into Standards V and VI from all over the old Ekiti District, including Akure and Igbara-Oke in the old Ondo Province. It was initially a Lower Middle School under the joint administration with the Emmanuel Primary School, Ado-Ekiti. The school premises then situated at the present Bishop's Court of the Ekiti Anglican Diocese in Ado-Ekiti. In the earlier days, the school hymn was *"Christ is the King, O friends rejoice"*. Later, it was *"Father of men in whom are one"*. It was Reverend Canon Leslie Donald Mason who changed the School hymn to *Christ is our corner stone*. It was christened "Christ's School" in 1936 by Governor Bourdillon and became a Middle School in 1942. Archdeacon Dallimore's vision was to provide a good quality education with Christian teachings for all God's children. A "national" rather than an "Ekiti" school, hence, male and female students from places beyond Ekiti State were enrolled. He was sustained and supported by his educationist wife, Dorothy. Venerable Archdeacon Henry Dallimore presented selected seven special students as external candidates for Cambridge examinations in 1945 and they all passed excellently. It was their success that revealed the potentials of the school to the government and was allowed in 1947 to proceed into a full-fledged secondary school. Venerable Dallimore left in 1947. Reverend Canon Mason was the only

Archdeacon Henry Dallimore (1885-1970)
Founder/High Master 1933-1937

university graduate when he assumed duty as the principal in 1948 and he developed the institution fully into a secondary school of promise. He presented the first set of "official" graduates in 1948. Christ's School products dominated government scholarships usually awarded on merit by the federal government in respect of the University of Ibadan entrance examination to the preliminary classes in the nineteen fifties and sixties. In a particular year, Christ's School products won eight out of the usual ten awards.

The system was sustained until Canon Mason, with a different disposition to coeducational programme, assumed duty as the principal in 1948. In the early 1960s, the first set of HSC students were admitted. The administration of the Boys' and Girls' schools was merged in 1966 when Chief R. A. Ogunlade, the first alumnus to be appointed the school principal, took charge. He was transferred out of the school in 1973, subsequent to the takeover by government. The take-over brought political interference to the school administration and ultimately led to the downward trend in the standard of the school. The Boys' and Girls' sections of the school emerged in 1979 with the change of government, after thirteen years of a merged school.

The transfer of Venerable R.A. Ogunlade in January 1973, expectedly came with implications. It brought another dimension to the level of commitment to the management of the school. His case was first of its kind as a former student, who became a teacher and the first indigenous principal. Politics crept into school administration system of the old south western states in Nigeria. The climax of the downward trend that took its toll on the affairs of the school was between late 1970s and early 1980s. The end of the political era in December 1983 gave a kind of new vista for the school which encouraged old students to step-in and they started supporting the school administration. The era of having a principal for the junior school and another one for the senior classes later had its own repercussion until it was reversed through a policy review by the state government.

Canon Leslie Donald Mason (9/9/1908-1985) Principal 1948-1966

Dallimore founded the School; Mason consolidated and gave it the national vista, while Ogunlade brought an indigenous flare to the school. It is therefore no surprise, that from the late 1950, especially in the 1960s till present, you will find Christ's School alumni and alumnae in the highest echelon of all endeavours – university professors, senior government officials, top company executives etc. Virtually every old generation set has produced various distinguished Nigerians. Kudos to everyone who made Christ's School, the institution it has become. The Church Missionary Society founded the school and saw to the sustenance of excellence; strong christian values and ethics were paramount. The good thing is that the Mission, Anglican Diocese of Ekiti regained ownership of the school. The location of the school on the crest of Agidimo Hill with an uncommon landscape, complemented with distinct structures built with stones on a large expanse of land make the school a beautiful architecture master piece, soothing to behold. The ambiance of the school premises is welcoming for new students, which aids studying and acclimatisation to the Christ's School culture. At the peak of its glory, Christ's School's academic excellence was its forte, having repeatedly produced some of the best results at WASC, among the league of secondary schools in the country. Venerable Henry Dallimore will be remembered as the person who put up the early mud and stone buildings; while the Reverend Canon L. D. Mason, whose students gave the title of "The Builder", put up the wonders of all the stone blocks. He also, a branding grandmaster produced the timeless Christ's School logo which was formally introduced to the school documents between 1949 and 1950. Venerable R. A. Ogunlade takes credit for the cement block buildings, while Chief Olusola Bayode was noted for the red bricks. The old students, having turned out well in their various careers often remain in lasting gratitude to the founder, the builders and the resourceful teachers.

The school houses/dormitories were "conclaves of fraternity". The Houses - Babamboni (Red), named after the first notable indigenous missionary; Dallimore (Green), after the founder of the school; Mason formerly Bishop, (Blue), after the consolidator and Harding (Yellow), after the first European Church Missionary Society missionary in Ekiti. Naming of the houses after the early missionaries and the founder of the school was mooted in 1939. The school chapel was formally commissioned on February 5th, 1947; a date chosen by the then Ekiti District Church Council, to honour the founder, who was born in England on the same day in 1885. The chapel has become part of the legacies the alumni of the school cherish.

All Students of old must learn to sing at least the first and the last stanzas of a considerable number of hymns from the Songs of Praise or Ancient and Modern.

As an institution whose foundation is in Christ, the boarding students pray collectively 10 times daily, Monday to Friday, as a tradition. A typical day starts with morning devotion in all the dormitories, prayer is said before and after all three meals in the dining hall, prayer at the school chapel before classes and after evening classes. The 10th prayer is said before going to bed. The official school prayer remains unchanged and it is as relevant as ever to the essence of founding the school. *"Grant us O Lord; that this school will be a Christian school; not in name only, but in deed and in truth; in the name of Christ, whose name we bear, amen"*. In addition to academic performance which made

Christ's School to tower among contemporary secondary schools of the time, is in the fact that the school was a leader in sports.

The alumni rekindled interest of old students in the school with **Chief A. S. Asebiomo**, the pioneer Alumni President (1979-82). He was succeeded by **Archdeacon R. A. Ogunlade** (1982-1995); **Justice Olajide Olatawura** led (1995-2008). **Prince Bisi Aladejana** (2009); **Dr Kayode Obembe** (2009-2012); **Chief Mrs Fadeke Alabi** (2012-2015); **Dr Uduimo Justus Itsueli** was the president in 2015-2020 and was succeeded by **Kunle Jinadu**.

The Alumni Chapters in the United Kingdom and United States of America as well as alumni branches in Lagos, Ibadan, Abuja, Ado-Ekiti, Port Harcourt and Osogbo have been working hard collectively to give back to their alma mater. After the 1983 intervention, the national alumni body ensured financial and material support to the aid of the school. Consequently, the alumni association gave the school a new Library Block/Hall of Fame, while two class sets built a block each of three and two classrooms respectively. These are apart from the various donations in cash and kind, coming from individuals, class sets and branches.

The annual Reunion and Homecoming of old students in Ekiti was conceived in the USA in 2005; aiming to bring together old students, from within and outside the country, to Ado-Ekiti to fraternize and raise funds for the school. The first Reunion in December 2006 was organized and funded by a multi-set group led by Baba-Ijo Ogunkua. Thereafter, Reunions and Homecomings were based on "passing-the-torch" concept, whereby chapters, branches and national alumni volunteer to host the event. The second, third, fourth and fifth Reunions and Homecomings in 2007, 2008, 2011 and 2012 were hosted by 1965-1969/71 set; 1966-1970/72 set; Christ's School Alumni Association North America and the UK Chapters respectively. The 6th Reunion and Homecoming which fell on the 80th anniversary celebration in 2013, was hosted by the Lagos Branch of the alumni association under the leadership of Mr. Yemi Akeju. The 7th Reunion was held in 2014 while the 8th was in 2015 by 1971-1975 set. The 9th Homecoming was hosted by the 1972-1976 set, while subsequent homecomings till date were hosted by sets that marked milestones of graduating from the great school.

TIMELINE OF LANDMARKS FROM 1933 TO 2022

1933: The School started as a Lower Middle School at the present Ekiti Anglican Bishop's Court premises, Ado-Ekiti.

1934: As early as 1934, it was visible that the total impact of the education given was to make the individual a useful person to himself and to his community.

1936: In June 1936 the school moved to its permanent site on the crest of Agidimo Hill, Ado-Ekiti. On August 6th 1936, the Governor of Nigeria, Sir Bourdillon visited the school, on which occasion the name was changed to Christ's School.

1937: The Superintendent of Education in Ondo Province wrote: "*The tone and discipline of the School are very good and altogether; this is one of the pleasantest Schools I have seen*"

1940: Three dormitories were built and were named Block A, B & C which later became

Harding House (Yellow), Babamboni House (Red) and Dallimore House (Green) respectively. Bishop House (Blue) was later built and named after Mason. In 1940 the Senior Education Officer, Owo and Benin Provinces wrote "*This is the best School I have yet seen in Nigeria*"

1943: Christ's School grew as a secondary school in stages, it moved up to Class IV in 1943.

1944: The High Master, Archdeacon Dallimore created a class of seven brilliant boys that he prepared for the Cambridge School Certificate Examination.

1945: Agriculture and cattle-keeping were included in the school programme. Likewise, Carpentry, Masonry and Gardening on every Crafts-Day (Wednesday). In 1945 the students presented for external examination passed with six in Grade II and one in Grade III.

1946-49: Students participated in the building of the School Chapel, new hostels, classrooms, new laboratories-and staff houses, all in granite stone masonry

1947: The Chapel was formally commissioned on February 5, 1947. February 5 was chosen in honour of the founder, Venerable Dallimore who was born same day in 1885, in

England. Dallimore left in 1947, Chief E. A. Babalola acted as High Master for 6 months period of interregnum and Rev Canon L. D. Mason stepped into office as Principal in January 1948. The ship that brought Canon Mason berthed in Lagos on Friday, 17th August, 1945 and he was met in Ibadan the following day by Leslie Murphy and his first tour of duty at Igbobi College had started. He completed a first tour of some two years on the staff of Igbobi College, where he was appointed a House Master and during this time, the school moved back to Lagos. Rev Canon L. D. Mason stepped into office as Principal of Christ's School in January 1948.

1948: The official first set of the Senior Cambridge School leavers was produced. The officially recognized set of Senior Cambridge School Certificate candidates sat for their papers at Ilesha in Academic excellence reached its peak under Reverend Canon L. D. Mason (1948-66).

A small electricity generator was installed in 1948 by Mason, there was none in the whole of Ado Township then and the school always stood tall over the hills at night.

1949: Science Laboratories were built using students labour. Additional Mathematics, Biology, Chemistry, Fine Arts, Physics, Technical Drawings and Zoology became part of the curriculum.

1950

1950: The School crest was formerly introduced to the school documents between 1949 and 1950 by the "Brand Master", Canon Mason. Mr Ben Oluwole was among the students in the Library with him when he got the inspiration for the original concept of the timeless school emblem.

1952: Reverend Canon Mason got approval for The School as a Cambridge recognized centre for school certificate examinations.

1954: The last set of students writing School Certificate Examinations in Form VI and the first set writing the examinations in Form V sat jointly for the examinations.

1955: The Anglican Girls' School was established, opposite the Agidimo Hill site of the Christ's School, Ado-Ekiti.

1958: 28 students passed with Grade I, 15 in Grade II and 4 in Grade III

1966: On retirement of Canon Mason, Venerable R. Akinloye Ogunlade stepped in as Principal of Christ's School. The same year, the Ekiti Anglican Girls Grammar School merged with Christ's School

1968: Between 1968 and 1970, the school Post Office was built and the road from gate to Principal's office was tarred with active participation of the students.

1975: Christ's School won the Principal's Cup in 1975

Students in the school farm with Canon Mason in the early 1960s

1978: Akinjide Ogunjobi HSC 78-79/085 and Akosile HSC 78-79/282 composed an anthem which was common among the later day and new generation of old students; *Christ's School is the place amongst mountains....*

1979: After 13 years as a mixed school, the Girls section was separated from the boy's School and named Christ's Girl's School, while the boy's section simply remained as Christ's School.

1980: Canon L. D. Mason made a return visit to Nigeria.

1984: Christ's School had the boarding facility restored in September 1980 after the systematic but gradual scheme of closing down boarding facilities all over old Ondo State and other states in the old western region.

1985/86: The first intervention project by Old Students by refurbishing the old Form I Classroom, which was dilapidating. It was embarked upon by the 1956-60 set and commissioned by Governor Mike Akhigbe of Ondo State. Other sets have followed ever since. HSC Programme was reintroduced into Christ's School and two other schools in Ondo State. The system closed down in 1990 with the introduction of the 6-3-3-4 Education System in Nigeria.

1988: Commissioning by Canon L. D. Mason of the ultra-modern School Library built in place of the semi-circular flower bed, a project jointly financed by the School (majorly), students labour, the PTA and old students, mainly the 1957 Set that paid for the cost of Canon Mason's flight to Nigeria. That was Canon Mason's last visit to Nigeria. The year also witnessed the tarring of the main driveway again, which was commissioned by Governor Ernest Adeleye, an old student, then Governor of Rivers State.

1989: Canon L. D. Mason passed away. His ashes were brought by Chief S.B. Falegan from Sheffield, U.K. and interred on the grounds of the School Chapel, an occasion celebrated in the typical Yoruba way of celebrating the passage of community Titans.

1991: Christ's School won for keeps the Ondo state Principal's Cup football competitions on winning the Cup that year for the third consecutive year 1989, 1990 and 1991.

1992: The shopping complex built with School fund, assisted with student labour was commissioned.

1995: Venerable Rufus Akinloye Ogunlade, first African Principal of the School, earlier a Teacher, Sports Master, Vice-Principal, died and his body was interred on the grounds of the School Chapel.

2001: Commissioning of the "Ghana House" a donation to the School by an Alumnus Olusola Luther-King (Olusola Alagbe)

2009: Commissioning of the Alumni Hall, a block whose foundation was laid in 1969, meant to be a School Assembly Hall, but which remained abandoned until 2009 when the Old Students Association took over, completed it to finish and named it Alumni Hall.

2010: Total refurbishing of the School Chapel which was supervised by Chief SB Falegan and the Dining Hall were completed as Alumni Projects. The Anglican Bishop of Ekiti, Most Rev'd S. A. Abe rededicated the buildings on completion. Also, in 2010, a block of dormitory was presented to the Girls' Section by Dr. Kayode Obembe, onetime Alumni National President.

2013: The 80th Anniversary of the School was celebrated with grandeur, by which time the Alumni Association had been playing decisive roles. Seye Adetunmbi packaged a book titled "In Deed and in Truth"; the publication was sponsored by Lagos Branch of the Alumni Association to mark 80th anniversary of founding Christ's School.

2015 Sir Uduimo Justus Itsueli was elected the President of the Alumni Association and the new EXCO was inaugurated in March 2016.

2016 Alumni raised fund to fence the premises of Girls Section of the School. On 26/8/16, the Alumni President led the delegation to Chief Ayo Fayose, the Governor of Ekiti-State

2017: The report of the working committee of Christ's School was concluded and the proposal to Ekiti State Government for the handover of the school was submitted. The gate of main campus was built by 1973-77 set to mark their 40 years of graduation.

2018: Handover proposal was presented to the state government

2019: Ekiti State Government under the leadership of Dr Kayode Fayemi formally handed over Christ's School to the Anglican mission in Ekiti in September 2019.

2020: Kunle Jinadu was elected the alumni president in the first electronic voting by the alumni body and will go down as the best election held so far by the alumni association

2021: Three sets held their homecoming. 1975-80 set hosted tarred the road to the two school compounds and build the gate for the Girls' section. Members of the HSC 1978-1980 and 1979-1981 donated furniture and laboratory equipment to the school.

2022: Hybrid group of 1978 and 1979 HSC sets hosted Homecoming in April 2022.

Christ's School 1st Eleven of the soccer team in the 1960s when Macaulay Iyayi (middle, squatting) was the Goalkeeper. Chief R.A. Ogunlade (sitting 1st from left)

THE PAST PRINCIPALS OF CHRIST'S SCHOOL

The Headmasters, High Masters and Principals 1933-2022

The *Headmasters* of Ekiti Central School were:

a. Mr. A. A. Oyenuga who was headmaster in 1933
b. Prince J. O. Alade 1934-1937
c. Rev T. V. Aderinola in 1938
d. Mr. G.A. Ogunyomi 1939- 1942

High Masters

e. Venerable Henry Dallimore used the High Master January 1943-May 1947
f. Chief E.A. Babalola High Master, July-December 1947

Principals

g. Canon Leslie Donald Mason, Principal January 1948-1966
h. Chief Rufus Akinloye Ogunlade 1967-1972
i. Rev J.B.P. Lafinhan, January 197-1974
j. Chief E. A. Olugboja, Acting Principal January 1974-January 1975
k. Mr. Ade Fasoro, February-August 1975
l. Chief R. F. Fasoranti, 1975–1978
m. Mr. S.O. Agbebi 1978-1984
n. Chief Olusola Bayode 1984-1994
o. Mr Kehinde Ojo 1995-2006
p. Elder M. A. Fasanmade May 2006-December 2007
q. Mr. Ade Olomofe, January 2008-January 2010
r. Prince Adewole Akinyede Principal in 2010-2014
s. Mr. Tanwa Oyebode   2005-2009 (Junior School)
t. Mr C. A. Abe 2014-2019
u. Dr Kunle Babalola 2019-2021
v. Canon Olurotimi Oso 2021-

The Venerable Archdeacon and Mrs. H. Dallimore

Ekiti Anglican Girl's Grammar School (EAGSS)/Christ's Girl's School (CGS)
1. Mrs C. O. Akinla   1955-1956
2. Mrs Y. Reed   1957-1963

Christ's Girl's School

1. Miss S. H. Davis — 1979-1983
2. Mrs. A. O. Owoeye — 1983-1986
3. Mrs. E. M. Ofere — 1986-1987
4. Mrs. F. A. Arikembi — 1987-1991
5. Chief Mrs. A. A. Ajibulu — 1991-2001
6. Chief Mrs. B. A. Balogun — 2001-2004
7. Chief Mrs. M. O. Adeniran — 2004-2006
8. Chief Mrs. M. O. Fasuan — 2006-2011
9. Mrs. M. I. Ogunrinde — 2011-2015
10. Mrs. I. M. Olonisakin — 2006-2011 (Junior School)
11. Mrs. C. M. Onipede — 2015-2019
12. Chief Mrs Remi Agbaje-Esan — 2019 -

The Past Principals 1933-2022

Ven. H. Dallimore
High Master 1933-1947

Chief E. A. Babalola
Acted July – Dec.1947

Canon L.D. Mason
Principal 1948-1966

Ven R. A. Ogunlade
1966-1972

Rev JBP Lafinhan
1973-74

Mr T. Ade Fasoro
Feb-August 1975

Chief E.O. Olugboja
Acting 1974-75

Chief R. F. Fasoranti
1975-1978

Chief Agbebi
1978-1984

Chief Bayode
1984-1994

Mr Kehinde Ojo
1995–2006

Mr M.A. Fasanmade
May 2006–Dec. 2007

Mr Ade Olomofe
2008-2010

Prince Wole Akinyede
2010-2014

Mrs Idowu Ogunrinde
Girls' School 2011-2015

Akinlolu Abe
2014 - 2019

Dr Adekunle Babalola
2019-2021

Mrs C.M. Onipede
Girls' section 2019-2019

Chief Mrs Remi Esan
Girls' section 2019

Canon Rotimi Oso
Principal 2021

School Volley Ball Team that won a national Trophy. Mr Fagbemi Sports Master (L), Mr Agbebi standing right, next to Segun Aganga, while Olubunmi Famosaya

Net Ball Champions, Mrs Tinu Emiola nee Agbede standing in the center

Some of the Eminent Old Students

Chief J. E. Babatola

Chief D. O. Adetunmbi

Prof J.F. Ade Ajayi

Maj-Gen R. A. Adebayo

Chief Hector Omoba

Prof Sam Aluko

Chief A. S. Asebiomo

Chief Mrs Oyin Ade-John

Oba Adegoke Adegboye

Right Rev. Olajide

Chief Samuel Asabia

Chief Jonathan M. Akinola

Chief Deji Fasuan   Justice O. Olatawura   Prof Adelola Adeloye   Prof Ajibola Taylor

Dr Chris Kolade   Prof K. Osuntokun   Architect Fola Alade   Dr Elkanah Adesokan

Rt. Rev. Elijah Ogundana   Prof Jide Osuntokun   Prof Israel Owolabi   Prof Banji Akintoye

Chief S. B. Falegan Justice M. A. Borisade Prof Bolaji Akinyemi Prof M. A. Omolewa

Prof Ajibola Meshida Prof Mrs Similolu Afonja Prof L. Adamolekun Prof Akin Oyebode

Prof Niyi Osundare Dr U. Justus Itsueli Macaulay Iyayi Baba-Ijo Segun Ogunkua

Prof Modupe Adelabu   Moyo Ajekigbe   Prof Femi Oyebode   Dr Erastus Akingbola

Soji Awogbade   Sesan Ogunro   Bayo Osibo   Prof Bolaji Aluko

Dr. Dokun Adedeji   Yemi Akeju   Segun Aganga   Gbenga Oyebode

Yemi Farounbi   Mrs Nike Babatola Prof Adesuyi Ajayi   Engr. Dayo Adetunmbi

Mrs Wura Ajayi   Prince Dapo Abiodun   Mofe Akinbanji   Justice Kunle Adeleye

Col. Deji Okeya Rtd   Mrs Kemi Ajayi   Dr J. K. Fayemi   Ambassador Eniola Ajayi

4.4. ILESA GRAMMAR SCHOOL

Ilesa Grammar School, formerly known as Ijesa High School, was established in 1934. The journey started on the 9th of April in 1924 during one of the meetings of Egbe Atunluse, the founding proprietor when a motion laying emphasis on educational matters in Ijesa, was moved. Ten years after, the school took off on 50 acres land following the decisive steps taken by Egbe Atunluse. It is the oldest secondary school in Ijesa land and second oldest in Osun State. The school developed to be among the prestigious AIONIAN institutions. The early principals were Rev. E. C. Doherty Nicholas, Rev. N. O. A. Lahanmi and Canon Akinyemi. The debut entrance examination was conducted on the 18th of January 1934 and 21 boys were the pioneer students. Classes commenced informally on Monday, 29th of January in 1934 while the school was formally commissioned on Monday 5th of February in 1934 by the District Officer for Ife/Ilesa District, Capt. J. A. Mackenzie.

Reverend Lahanmi and some teachers of Ilesha Grams in 1952

Among the prominent products of the school were Justice Kayode Eso, Pastor Enoch Adejare Adeboye, Justice Salihu Modibbo Alfa Belgore, Justice Emmanuel Araka, Dr. Festus Ajayi, Justice Egbert Udo Udoma, Dr. Jaja Anucha Wachukwu, Venerable L. L. Eso, Emmanuel Asaolu Fafowora, Ezekiel Aofolajuwonlo, John Aoko, Enoch Ayeni, Gabriel Aluko-Oluokun, Habibu Karimu, Samuel Doherty, Adolphous Doherty, Eric Mabayoje, Messrs Banjo Fasuyi, Ayo Oni, Folorunso Obembe, Professor Iyiola Jegede, Alhaji Kayode Animasaun, Justice Tunde Ilori, Chief Oladipo Fadahunsi, Kayode Hanid, Diran Oyeleye, Yinka Fajemisin, Ibukun Fajemisin, Samuel Okagbue, Ellis Ojunta, Owen Fiebai Okokorobiko,

Justice Kayode Eso

Pastor E. Adeboye

Justice Alfa Belgore

Justice Emmanuel Araka

Justice Udo Udoma

Ven L. L. Eso

Dr Jaja Wachukwu   Prof Iyiola Jegede

Justice Tunde Ilori

Ayo Oni

Akin Fafowora

4.5. EDO COLLEGE, BENIN CITY

Edo College in Benin-City, is the oldest secondary grammar school in the Mid-Western Region. It was established in February 1937 and started as the Benin Middle School with forms I, II and III. In April 1937, the school enrolled 76 students and moved from the temporary site at the old Government School, Benin City to the Idia College premises. In 1973, the school relocated to its present site along Murtala Mohammed Way, Benin City. Some of the prominent old students include King Ewuare II of Benin, Arthur Okowa Ifeanyi, Tom Ilube, Chris Okotie, Lucky Igbinedion, James Ibori and Obi Olloh.

Oba Ewuare II of Benin   Lucky Igbinedion   Arthur Okowa   James Ibori

Tom Ilube   Obi Olloh   Chris Okotie

CHAPTER FIVE

THE 4ᵀᴴ DECADE IN THE 20ᵀᴴ CENTURY: 1941-1950

5.1.   REAGAN MEMORIAL BAPTIST GIRLS SCHOOL, LAGOS

Reagan Memorial Baptist Girls' Secondary School was established by the Baptist Christian Mission. It started as a co-educational primary school in 1941 and was named after Miss Lucille Reagan who had the vision of establishing a Baptist school for the complete training of girls in all conventional fronts. It later became a girls' school and Miss Cora Ney Hardy; a Baptist Missionary came in 1947 to head the school and introduced a boarding school system. In 1952, the secondary education commenced. The primary and the secondary school remained in the same compound until the primary school relocated to Onike in 1988. Two dormitories, a dining hall with kitchen were built in 1958. The houses were named after Dr. H. C. Geomer and Cora Ney Hardy while the dining hall was named Mrs. J. T. Ayorinde. Like other schools in Lagos-State, the government took over the administration of the school in 1979. It was returned in August 2001 to the Nigerian Baptist Convention. The school has produced so many notable Nigerians. Some of the alumni include Mrs M. R. A. Adeleke, Mrs Ayo Ogunade, Mrs Olabowale Adetunmbi, Mrs Yeside Oyetayo, Mrs Abi Peter Thomas, Mrs Subulola Fashina, Mrs Busola Oshinusi.

Some members of 1977-1982 set

Mrs M. R. A. Adeleke

5.2.   LISABI GRAMMAR SCHOOL, ABEOKUTA

Lisabi Grammar School was established in 1943, in Abeokuta in Ogun-State. It is a coeducational public high school situated at Idi Aba, Abeokuta. Among the prominent old students were Chief Bode Akindele, Simeon Borokini, Tunde Lemo, Lekan Salami, Tunde Bakare, Reuben Abati, Samson Adeola Odedina and Funmi Babington-Ashaye.

Chief Bode Akindele   Chief Lekan Salami Rt Rev Simeon Borokini Samson A. Odedina

Tunde Lemo   Pastor Tunde Bakare Dr Reuben Abati   Funmi Babington-Ashaye

5.3.   OFFA GRAMMAR SCHOOL, OFFA 1943

Offa Grammar School (OGS) was founded in 1943 through the concerted efforts of Offa Descendants Union. The union was an initiative of Offa indigenes in Lagos between 1935 and 1938. In 1940, the descendants' union raised fund for a community-owned secondary school to be established in Offa. When Mr S. O. Ajayi was the principal and Rev R. N. Ludlow was the chairman of the Board of Governors, the school moved to the permanent site in January 1945. There were 65 students managed by a staff of 8 in 1946 and subsequent to the Thorburn-inspection, the school was approved Junior Cambridge examination. Rev J. B. Olafimihan was the 2nd school principal till 1949 when Mr T. A. Babalola became the acting Principal; while the substantive principal, Mr J. A. Osanyin assumed office in September 1949.

Rev R. N. Ludlow

Some of the prominent products of the school include Chief Okobi, Prof. Mosobalaje O. Oyawoye, Justice M. S. Alfa Belgore, Oba Oladele Olashore, Chief Oluwafemi Olukanmi, General Alani Akinrinade, Dr Remi Oni, Dele Belgore SAN, Prince Tayo Popoola, Dele Bello SAN, Lateef Fagbemi SAN, Yinka Adeyemi, AIG Kayode Aderanti rtd, AIG Fimihan Adeoye rtd and Kayode Alabi.

Oba Oladele Olashore   Gen. Alani Akinrinade   Prof M. O. Oyawoye   Justice M. S. Belgore

Dr Remi Oni   Mrs Bolanle Oni   AIG Fimihan Adeoye rtd   Yinka Adeyemi a.k.a. 2A

Soji Oyeyipo SAN   Soji Oyeleke SAN   Dele Belgore SAN   Prof Olawale Okeniyi

Prince Tayo Popoola   AIG Kayode Aderanti rtd   Dele Bello   Kayode Alabi

78

5.4. OLIVET BAPTIST HIGH SCHOOL, OYO

Olivet Baptist High School, Oyo was founded by the American Southern Baptist Mission on the 29th of January in 1945. The school started in the premises of the old Baptist mission house at Oke-Isokun in Oyo city, where Rev. Pinnock, the first Baptist missionary to the ancient Oyo empire established a mission post. The succeeding principals of the school over the years were Mrs. J. C. Powell, 1946; Deacon T. A. Okanla, Headmaster 1945-1952; Rev. Carl F. Whirley, 1948; Rev. W. Joel Fergeson, 1948-1951; Rev. J. B. Durham, Acting Principal 1951; Rev. M. L. Garrett, Acting Principal 1952-1953; Mr. E. A. Iyanda, Acting Principal 1955-1957; Rev. Homer A. Brown, 1957-1962; Rev. J. B. P. Lafinhan, 1962-1972; Chief R. F. Fasoranti, 1973-1975; Chief S. O. Omitade, 1975-1977; Chief J. I. Popoola, 1977-1982; Mr. I. A. Adisa, 1982-1989; Mr. A. A. Adeniran, 1990-1994; Mr. A. A. Adeniji, 1994-2000; Mr. S. O. Okegbenle, 2000-2002; Mrs. F. M. Taiwo, 2002, and Mrs O. Dosunmu came on board in 2019. The school, popularly called Olivet Heights has produced many prominent Nigerians.

Yomi Ajayi   Tunde Busari SAN   Chief Ayo Fayose

5.5.   HOLY CHILD COLLEGE, IKOYI, LAGOS

Holy Child College in Ikoyi, Lagos was established in 1945. It was founded by the society of the Holy Child Jesus on the 9th of April in 1945 and the college started with thirty students and four nuns. Founding of the school was an initiative attributed to Archbishop Leo Taylor who wanted a good secondary education for girls in his archdiocese. The Society of the Holy Child Jesus was founded by Rev. Mother Cornelia Cornnelly in 1846 in England. The College has produced many prominent women in Nigeria amongst whom were: Mrs Yetunde Francesca Emmanuel nee Pereira, Dr Yewande Jinadu nee Emiabata, Mrs Bola Adesola nee Lardner, Mrs Titi Akisanya, Mrs Ibijoke Sanwoolu, Yinka shittabey, Mrs Yemisi Openiyi nee Ibidapo-Obe, Kemi Awodein, Mrs Bimbo Jijoho Ogun nee Sule

Mrs Francesca Emmanuel

Dr Yewande Jinadu

Mrs Bola Adesola

Mrs Titi Akisanya

Mrs Joke Sanwoolu

80

5.6. OUR LADY OF APOSTLES SECONDARY SCHOOL, LAGOS

Our Lady of Apostles Secondary School, Yaba, Lagos was established in 1956. It was built by the Catholic missionary sisters as an all-girls school. The school is noted for its moral and academic excellence over the years.

The school has produced many successful and respectable personalities in Nigeria. Some of the alumni include Dr Christiana Ogbogu, Dora Amahian, Yinka Ogunde, Sanny Almedia, Dr Helen Ekwuweme, Dora Odah, Cosma & Damiana, Rosemary Chimezie, Deaconess Philomena Onoyeme Disu-Edevbaro, Dr Adetoun Dipeolu, Funke Adekoya, Josephine Effah-Chukwuma, Kikelomo Bukola Odeyemi Ayeye, Mrs Olubunmi Grace Ajoke Johnson, Mrs Adenike Iyoha.

Funke Adekoya SAN   Bunmi JohnsonPhil   Philomena Disu-Edevbaro   Yinka Ogunde

Dr Christiana Ogbogu   Dr Suyi Park   Ladies of OLA – The Great OLARIANS

Kikelomo Ayeye   Bimbola Jelugbo   Cosma and Damiana   Nike Iyoha nee Akapo

CHAPTER SIX

THE 5TH DECADE IN THE 20TH CENTURY: 1951-1960

6.1. TITCOMBE COLLEGE, EGBE

Titcombe College (TC) is a secondary school established in Egbe, Kogi-State on the 26th of January in 1951. The school was founded by missionaries of the Sudan Interior Mission. TC has produced notable Nigerians including Vice-Admiral Samuel Afolayan, Professor Pius Adesamni, Professor Solomon Adebola and Tunji Arosanyin.

Vice-Admiral Samuel Afolayan

Prof Pius Adesanmi

Prof Solomon Adebola

6.2.   ST. THOMAS'AQUINAS COLLEGE, AKURE

St. Thomas Aquinas College, Akure) was established in January 1951. It was named after a patron saint, St. Thomas of Aquinas (1225 to 1274). Aquinas College as it is popularly called was founded by the Catholic Diocese of Ondo under the leadership of The Most Rev. Thomas Hughes. The school started formally on the 27th of January in 1951 with a class of 34 boys.

Members of St Eugene's House in 1967

There are so many prominent Nigerians who are products of the college.

Sir Olubunmi Famosaya   Kunle Ekundayo   Prof Sesi Ajayi-Vincent

84

Tayo Jegede SAN   Boyede Ekundayo a.k.a. Arena Classical

The photograph of the 1971 Aquinas College football team, at the Liberty Stadium, Ibadan, just before the epic final against Loyola College, Ibadan. L-R: Adetoro, Akinwole (007), Bobona, Luke Eromosele, Shittu, Adenika, Agoro, Segun Egenus, Benedict Popoola, Sagalo, Uche Okoro. Madu Oko the Goal Keeper, stooping

85

6.3.   QUEEN'S SCHOOL, IBADAN

Queen's College, Ibadan was established by the government of the Western Region to commemorate the ascension of Queen Elizabeth II, the Queen of England in 1952 in order to further expand the scope of female education in Nigeria. Four pioneering students and teachers moved from Queen's College Lagos to Ede the then location of the new Queen's School. Forms II to V moved to Ede and the pioneering principal was Miss E. Hobson. On February 16, 1952, the first set of Form I students joined the school to complete the five classes. Queen's School, Ede was relocated to Ibadan in 1967. The school was temporarily accommodated at Ransome Kuti College of Education, Apata for the junior classes and Olunloyo College of Education, for the senior classes during the tenure of Mrs R. M. Dunn as the Principal. The school moved to the permanent site at Apata-Ganga, with Mrs C. F. Oredugba as the Principal. Prominent alumnae include Dr Taiwo Adamson, Dr Ameyo Stella Adadevo, Dr Ogunsanya, Oyinda Ogunleye, Yinka Otukpe.

Dr A. Stella Adadevoh   Dr Taiwo Adamson   Oyinda Ogunleye   Pastor Yinka Otukpe

6.4.   OYEMEKUN GRAMMAR SCHOOL, AKURE

Oyemekun Grammar School, was established in January 1953 in Akure the capital city of Ondo-State. The past principals of the include Chief B.F.A. Adinlewa, Rev R. A. Ogunlade, A. S. Asebiomo, Somo Aina, J.O. Olugasa, R. Falowo and S. Ayodele. The school has produced so many prominent Nigerians that include Prof Ladipo Adamolekun, Prof Meshida, Pharmacist Tunde Adelaja.

Prof Ladi Adamolekun   Prof Ajibola Meshida   Pharm. Tunde Adelaja   Wale Jegede

6.5.   URHOBO COLLEGE, EFFURUM

Urhobo College, Effurum was established by Urhobo Progressive Union in 1953. Effurum is close to Warri in Delta-State. Some of the well-known alumni include Prof. Tekena Tamuno and S. J. Okudu.

Prof Tekena Tamuno

6.6.   EKITI PARAPO COLLEGE, IDO-EKITI

Ekiti Parapo College (EPC) was established in 1954 through concerted efforts of the Ekiti National Association and Ekiti Progressive Union constituted by Ekiti indigenes resident abroad with the vision to establish the first community secondary school owned by Ekiti people. The school was formally commissioned with 25 pioneer students, the founding Principal and two teachers on August 5, 1954 by the then Hon. Minister of Education for Western Region of Nigeria, Chief S.O. Awokoya. The first principal of the school was Chief Adepoju Akomolafe and was ably assisted by Chief D.O. Adetunmbi (father of the author) and other pioneer teachers to give the college a good start. The succeeding principals over the years were Chief Alfred Siyanbola Asebiomo, 29/1/1954 to 30/41968, Mr. S. C. A. Yoloye 01/5/1968 to 2/1/1973, Chief Paul O. Oyeyemi 03/1/1973 to 31-Aug-1975, Chief J. A. Fasuba, 01/9/1975 to 31/8/1977, Mr. J. O. Alabi 01/9/1977 to 31/7/1978, Mr. S. V. K. Bamigboye 01/8/1978 to 14/9/1983, Chief L. O. Akinyede 15/9/1983 to 13/10/1986, Mr. J. A. Afolalu 14/9/1986 to 02/10/1997, Mr. J. A. Ogunlana 21/10/1997 to 23/6/1999, Chief Lanre Balogun 24/6/1999 to 10/11/1999, Chief Adewumi Fanilola 11/11/1999 to 30/9/2004, Chief Adewumi Fanilola (Snr school) 01/1/2004 to 19/9/2005, Mr. O. S. Gegeleso (Jnr school) 19/9/2004 to 05/4/2007, Mr. Yinka Pereao (Snr school) 19/9/2004 to 15/9/2011, Mr. O. T. Ogundipe (Snr school) 02/5/2007 to 30/9/2009, Mrs. M. A. Jaiyeoba 30/9/2009 to 08/7/2010, Mr. Tolu Ogunruku 09/7/2010 to 31/12/2013.

Some of the Past Principals

Chief Ade Akomolafe Chief Alfred S. Asebiomo Chief J.O. Alabi   Chief P. O. Oyeyemi

EPC has produced so many prominent Nigerians, some of them include Prof Afolayan, Senator Olubunmi Adetunmbi, Venerable Segun Agbetuyi, Pastor Yomi Sanya, Mrs Bose

Akingbade (nee Asebiomo), Segun Oluboyede, Tokunbo Oyeyemi, Dotun Adekanbi.

Chief Ade Akomolafe with some students of EPC in the 1960s

Mrs Yetunde Makinde   Tolu Ogunruku   Senator Olu Adetunmbi   Ayo Ogunruku

Ven Segun Agbetuyi   Abayomi Sanya   Mrs Bose Akingbade   Segun Oluboyede

89

6.7.   LOYOLA COLLEGE, IBADAN 1954

Loyola College, Ibadan (LCI) is a boys' only school, owned by the government of Oyo State. The school was founded by the Catholic Mission in 1954. It is located along the old Ife road in Agodi area of Ibadan metropolis. The college has produced so many prominent that include Lam Adesina, Chief Dele Fajemirokun, Oluwarotimi Odunayo Akeredolu, Raymond Dokpesi, Professor Patrick Utomi ,Prof Tunde Aderiye, Akin Fayomi, Folarin Latinwo, Dotun Akinola, Wale Adeniyi, Wale Osin, Dotun Adeniyi, Paul Toyin Olaleye, Dele Bakare, Oluseun Onigbinde, Lawson Oyekan, Oba Adeyeye Enitan Ogunwusi, Ekpo Una Owo Nta, Olumide Oyedeji.

Loyola College team in 1971

90

Alhaji Lam Adesina   Chief Dele Fajemirokun Dr Raymond Dokpesi Rotimi Akeredolu SAN

Prof Tunde Aderiye Prof Pat Utomi   Folarin Latinwo   Muyiwa Ayoade   Dotun Adeniyi

Dotun Akinola   Paul Olaleye   Wale Adeniyi   Ooni Enitan Ogunwusi

6.8. LAGOS ANGLICAN GIRLS GRAMMAR SCHOOL

Lagos Anglican Girls Grammar School was formally opened on the 27th of January in 1955 with a short service conducted by the Rev. Canon T. O. Dedeke. The school initially started at 17 Broad Street for a year. The founding principal was Mrs. Busola Olumide, nee Phillips and was in charge for 22 years. The following principal also served the school at various times: Mrs. A.O. Benson - August 1977 to July 1981, Mrs. O .O. Labode September 1981 to September 1998, Mrs. Y. A. Oguntona September 1998 to November 1999, Mrs. O. O. Carena November 1999 to September 2000, Mrs. A. D. Olumide September 2001 to December 2003, The Rev. T. Oduwole (Acting) January 2004 to September 2004, Mrs. M. Olukemi Akin-Ajayi September 2004 to November 2020 and Mrs F. Ogedengbe took charge in November 2020. Following the takeover of both primary and secondary schools by the government both at federal and state levels in the 1970s the religious organizations were no more in control of the schools they established. The standard of the school suffered setback until schools were returned to the original owners comprising of mission and private individuals after more than 25 years of the state government being in charge. In a letter dated 3rd of August in 2001, Lagos Anglican Girls' Grammar School was returned along with over forty other schools to their original owners by the Lagos State government. On the 2nd of October 2001, the school thankfully re-opened again under the management of the Anglican Mission with Mrs. Adeola Durotimi Olumide (an old girl of the school and former teacher) as the first principal after the interregnum.

Mrs Kemi Akin-Ajayi
Principal for 16 years

6.9.   MAYFLOWER SCHOOL, IKENNE

Mayflower School, Ikenne was founded by the renowned educationist, humanist, civil rights activist and social critic, Dr Tai Solarin. The school formally started with 70 students on the 27th of January in 1956. He was ably assisted by his beloved wife, Mrs Sheila Mary Tuer Solarin, a British woman and two children, Corrin and Tunde Solarin. The school is located on 90 acres of land at Ikenne in Ogun-State and the motto of the school is "Knowledge is Light" and the school uniform is styled after Tai Solarin's trademark of simple khaki shorts and short-sleeve shirts. Mayflower School manifested a very strong educational philosophy grounded in self-reliance, self-sacrifice, public service and physical activities. It is a mixed school with boarding facilities under a disciplined school administration of the legendary Dr Solarin who led by example and was the principal from 1956 to 1976. He structured the school to produce well rounded graduates from the school having exposed all the students to basic farming and other rudiments of a typical comprehensive and self-sustaining education. Consequently, the school was reputed for producing an outstanding quality graduates who have turned out well in their respective callings within and outside Nigeria. Some of the prominent old students include Oladapo Afolabi, William Kumuyi, Dayo Amusa, Richard Bamisile, Chude Jideonwo, Anthony Joshua, Pepenazi, Isio De-laVega Wanogho.

Dr. Tai Solarin

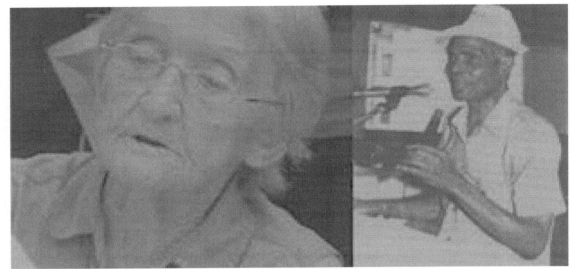

Dr & Mrs Tai Solarin

Pastor William Kumuyi Prof Oladapo Afolabi Dayo Amusa   Chude Jideonwo

SAINT FINBARR'S COLLEGE, LAGOS

St. Finbarr's College in Akoka, Yaba, Lagos was established by Rev Fr. D. J. Slattery, who came to Nigeria in 1939. The school was the first bilateral technical cum grammar school in the country and started with 6 students at St Paul's Catholic Primary School on Apapa Road, Ebute Metta. Fr Slattery eventually got 21 acres of virgin land in Akoka and the school moved to the permanent school site in 1959. The new site was officially opened by Dr Nnamdi Azikiwe, the First President of Nigeria in 1963. Rev Father Slattery was the school principal until the government took-over private schools in 1976. This was shortly after Fr Slattery finished 2-storey building for expansion of the technical department and introduction of electrical, basic electronics and auto-mechanics to the school curricular. For over two decades that the government took control of the college's management, it took toll on the high academic, moral, sports standards that St Finbarr's was noted for under the founder. At some point in 1979 when free education was introduced by the government, the compound of the college housed three schools - St. Finbarr's College, St. Finbarr's College 2 and Community Grammar School. Few years later, the two new schools were merged and named Akoka High School. In 2001, the school was returned to the catholic mission.

The school can boast of many distinguished Nigerians who passed through the college that include: Admiral Patrick Koshoni, Major General Cyril Iweze, Prince Deji Akinnubi, Cornelius Okoro, Moyo Onigbanjo SAN, Norrison Quakers SAN, Peter Amangbo, Commodore Kunlere, Stephen Keshi, Henry Nwosu, Nduka Ugbade, Prince Henry Amike, Segun Ajanlekoko, Pastor George Akhigbe.

Admiral Patrick Koshoni

Major-General Cyril Nweze

Norrison Quakers SAN

Segun Ajanlekoko

Prince Deji Akinnubi

Moyo Onigbanjo SAN

Stephen Keshi

Henry Nwosu

Nduka Ngbade

CHAPTER SEVEN

THE 1960S SECONDARY SCHOOLS

7.1.   FIWASAYE ANGLICAN GIRLS GRAMMAR SCHOOL, AKURE

Fiwasaye Anglican Girls' Grammar School, Akure was established in 1960. The Anglican Communion wanted a college for girls, to complement the already existing Boys' college, Oyemekun, Grammar School and Ms Rosa Jane Pelly, an English missionary, Oxford scholar and educator laboured for the take-off of the school as the founding and legendary principal for the first 13 years. She designed every building, planted every tree, chose every student, interviewed every teacher. She was committed to the school till the end and even after her transition because Fiwasaye was

Mama Rosa Jane Pelly

remembered in her will through Pelly Foundation. The school has produced wide range of women of repute in all spheres of human endeavours who have been deploying their resources to sustain the heritage of the great school. Prominent alumni of the school include Mrs Foluso Olayinka Onabowale, Mrs Pat Anabor, Mrs Funmi Adedibu, Prof Adenike Osofisan, Mrs Olufolake Oladunni Oyeyemi, Mrs Stella Kosemani Kolawole, Justice Opeyemi Oke, Princess Moradeke Ajibade, Tayo Daramola, Mrs Funwa Agbi, Mrs Jumoke Lambert, Mrs Modupe Dinyo, Gbolahan Daramola, Mrs Celia Ogunlesi.

97

Mrs Foluso Onabowale Justice Opeyemi Oke Mrs Kosemani Kolawole Mrs Folake O. Oyeyemi

Prof Nike Osofisan   Mrs Funmi Adedibu   Mrs Pat Anabor   Mrs Jumoke Lambert

Tayo Daramola   Princess Deke Ajibade Gbolahan Daramola   Mrs Celia Ogunlesi

7.2. METHODIST GIRLS HIGH SCHOOL, IFAKI

The need for a sister college in Ifaki resulted to the founding of a Girls High School by the Ifaki Circuit Methodist Church. Methodist Girls High School (MGHS) started in January 1961 and Miss BeuyI House was the first Principal. Rev D.A. Omotunde and Mrs Chopde were the legendary principals of the school for many years. MGHS has produced many women of substance within and outside Nigeria; some of them include: Mrs Olufunmilola Badejo, Mrs Alake Ajayi, Mrs Yemisi Arogundade Mrs Yetunde Makinde, Mrs Ojo, Mrs Dupe Olaiya, Mrs Yetunde Dada, Mrs Bolade Agbelese, Prof Titi Ufomata, Mrs Tokunbo Adeagbo, Justice Bisi Omoleye, Mrs Dupe Akinyemi, Regent Jumoke Mshelbwala, Mrs Foluso Akinyosoye, Dr Dayo Aladewolu, Mrs Iyabo Ogunsuyi, Mrs Funmi Balogun. Princess Duro Ojo, Mrs Nike Ogunyemi, Mrs Shade Afolabi, Mrs Yemisi

Mrs Chopde

Fasanmi, Mrs Tope Awe, Mrs Yetunde Comfort Green, Prof Bunmi Ajayi, Mrs Yinka Adanlawo, Mrs Bose Afolabi, Mrs Bunmi Latinwo-Ogunyemi, Mrs Bosipo Fagbuyi

Rev D. A. Omotunde, the Principal of Methodist Girls High School, Ifaki-Ekiti introduced the school prefects and staff to the Governor of Western Region, Major-General R. A. Adebayo on official visit to the school in 1968 to commission the science laboratories of the school.

Mrs Alake Ajayi   Mrs Anike Ojo   Mrs Yetunde Makinde   Mrs Yemisi Arogundade

Prof Titi Ufomata   Mrs Dupe Akinyemi   Regent J. Mshelbwala   Mrs Funmi Balogun

Princess Duro Ojo   Mrs C. Y. Green   Mrs Bunmi Ogunyemi   Mrs Bosipo Fagbuyi

7.3.   COMPREHENSIVE HIGH SCHOOL, AIYETORO

The old Western Region government established Comprehensive High School, Aiyetoro in Ogun-State of Nigeria in February 1963. The school is situated on a 171-hectare land, 37 kilometres west of Abeokuta. Apparently, one of the few secondary schools with such huge land acquisition as the time it was founded. The feat was able to be accomplished with the assistance from USAID through Harvard University that provided staffing resources and Ford Foundation that funded the school project until 1973. The school was primarily conceived by the authorities to meet the needs of manpower subsequent to the independence of Nigeria in 1960. It was a US Senator from New Jersey who proposed the establishment of Comprehensive High Schools in Nigeria and Kenya as a gateway of US influence in Africa. Compro as it is popularly called is a product of US international diplomacy through Educational AID and the Peace Corps of the JFK Administration. The physical project was given to USAID to execute and to administer for the first five years, while the academic staffing and curriculum activities were given to Harvard University with counterpart matching staff from the Western Nigeria educational ministry. Unequivocally, Comprehensive High School Aiyetoro at its peak became a model school in Nigeria. The school started with a dual educational system, the sixth form followed the British curriculum, while the junior school followed the American curriculum system. The plan for the American SAT exams as the terminal exam for the junior school had to be changed to WAEC after some years.

The succeeding principals over the years include Dr. John Sly 1963–1964, Chief J. B. O. Ojo 1964–1968, Dr. D. J. Bullock 1968–1970, Mr. L. A. Sofenwa 1970–1974, Dr. M. O. Alafe-Aluko 1974–1976, Mr. G. O. Kehinde 1976–1978, Mr. S. A. Ibikunle 1978–1982, Deacon G. O. Adekunte 1982–1986, Mr. J. O. Idowu 1986–1990, Chief P. A. Olaleye 1991–1995, Mr. T. O. Olanrewaju 1995–2001, Elder J. A. Idowu 2001–2007, Mr Morenikeji 2007–2008, Mr. F. Sawyer 2008–2012, Mr. O. Akinyinka 2012–2015 and Mr. S. S. Sekunmade came on board in 2015.

The school certainly made comprehensive education popular in Nigeria and has produced many prominent Nigerians that include Oba (Prof) Akinola Owosekun, Dr. Kunle Y. Adamson, Professor Oluwole Ajagbe, Dr. Olusegun Salako, Oluwarotimi Odunayo Akeredolu SAN, Mike Adenuga, Prof Adenike Osofisan, Prof. Abimbola Olowofoyeku, Prof Deji Adekunle, Gboyega/Tokunbo/Biola Fayemi, Dr Layi Oni, Mr. Kola Abiola, Dr. Prince Femi Debo-Omidokun,, Suraj Adekunbi, Olusegun Adewoye, Olufemi Oginni.

Chief M. Adenuga   Rotimi Akeredolu SAN Prof Adenike Osofisan   Prof A. Olowofoyeku

Abiola Fayemi   Dr Layi Oni   Prof Oluwole Ajagbe   Kola Abiola

7.4. INTERNATIONAL SCHOOL, IBADAN

International School Ibadan (ISI) was founded by Kurt Hahn, a German-British educator on the 13th of October in 1963. The establishment of the school was funded by USAID, Ford Foundation and the old Western Regional government through the donation of land. The pioneer teaching staff were mostly British expatriate educators from Gordonstoun in Scotland. The school is a co-educational with boarding facilities and day school window. It was primarily established to meet world-class educational standards for the children of expatriates, living and working in Nigeria, yet other wards were accommodated over the years. The first Principal was David S. Snell who was in charge from 1963 to 1965. The succeeding principals include Messrs John Gillespie 1965–1968, the legendary Archdeacon J. A. Iluyomade 1969–1985, the longest serving principal and the first Nigerian to head the school; Rev. (Dr.) Dapo Ajayi 1986–1988, Dapo Fajembola 1990–1991, Esther Adetola Smith 1991–2004, the first female principal; R.O. Akintilebo 2006–2007, Dr. M. B. Malik 2007–2017 and Phebean O. Olowe who came on board in 2017. The school song is:

> These things shall be
> A new generation,
> In every land,
> Of boys and girls shall stand,
> For brotherhood of man,
> Through service to mankind,
> And love for truth and peace,
> From ISI with one acclaim we pledge,
> Our faith in these....ISI!"

ISI has produced many distinguished Nigerians who include Prof Ngozi Okonjo-Iweala, Prof Yewande Olubummo, Omobola Johnson, Bolanle Austen-Peters, Mrs Bamidele Abiodun, Oluwatoyin Asojo, , Femi Emiola, Akin Fayomi, Toby Foyeh, Efa Iwara, Bill Ivy, Funmi Iyanda, Karen King-Aribisala, Tolu Ogunlesi, Alex Oke, Ifedayo Olarinde, Olayinka Omigbodun, Sasha P, Helen Prest-Ajayi (Miss Nigeria 1979), Joshua Uzoigwe

Prof Ngozi Okonjo-Iwela Prof Yewande Olubummo Mrs Omobola Johnson

Wale Oshin   Bolanle Austen-Peters   Tolu Ogunlesi

Christ's School, Ado-Ekiti

Government College, Ibadan

Ifaki Grammar School

Holy Child College

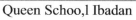

Queen Schoo,l Ibadan

106

St Anne's School   Titcombe College   Reagan Memorial Baptist

Government College Owerri

MBHS, Lagos

107

Staff of Barewa College

GCU

Aquinas College

CHAPTER EIGHT

8. THE NEW GENERATION HERITAGE SCHOOLS
An Overview of Federal Government Colleges and New Generation Schools

The federal government of Nigeria has always been funding establishment of schools in the country right from the colonial days. There are over a hundred federal government schools in Nigeria. For emphasis sake, the list of the secondary schools highlighted in this chapter is the Federal Government Colleges (FGC) established in virtually all the states within the federation of Nigeria. When the old generation heritage and premium schools were tiring out, and most of them were losing steam in terms of standard in all fronts, the federal colleges came to the rescue of parents seeking quality education for their children in a good academic environment with standard facilities. Ironically, the Nigerian factor crept into the management of the FGC, the schools suffered the fate of the of the old generation heritage schools, the facilities were depleted and most of them became a shadow of themselves. This development in the secondary school education in Nigeria led to the influx of the establishment of private premium secondary schools in Nigeria which only the rich could afford to send their children.

Apart from the few Federal government secondary schools that were established during the colonial days most of which were featured in the first five chapters of this book, the new federal government colleges were established from 1970s till the 21st century. The FGC includes:

South East Zone
1. Federal Girls Government College (FGGC), Umuahia in Abia-State
2. Federal Government College (mixed school), Ohafia in Abia-State
3. Federal School of Science and Technology (FSTC) mixed, Ohanso in Abia-State
4. FGC (mixed), Nise in Anambra-State
5. FGGC Onitsha in Anambra-State
6. FGC (girls only), FSTC (mixed) Awka in Anambra-State
7. FGC (mixed), Enugu

8. FGGC Lejja, in Enugu-State
9. FGC (mixed), Okigwe in Imo-State
10. FGGC Owerri in Imo-State
11. FSTC (mixed) Oguta in Imo-State
12. FGC (mixed) Okposi in Imo-State
13. FGGC Ezzamgbo in Imo-State
14. FSTC (mixed), Amuzu in Imo-State

North East Zone - Federal Unity Schools

15. FGC (mixed), Ganye in Adamawa-State
16. FGGC (mixed), Yola in Adamawa-State
17. FSTC (mixed), Michika in Adamawa-State
18. FGC (mixed), Azare in Bauchi-State
19. FGGC Bauchi
20. FGC (mixed), Maiduguri in Borno-State
21. FGGC Monguno in Borno-State
22. FSTC Lassa in Borno-State
23. FGC (mixed), Wukari in Taraba-State
24. FGGC Jalingo in Taraba-State
25. FSTC (mixed), Jalingo in Taraba-State
26. FGC (mixed), Buni-Yadi in Yobe-State
27. FGGC Potiskum in Yobe-State
28. FGC (mixed) Biliri in Gombe-State
29. FGGC Bajoga in Gombe-State (Girls Only)

South-South Zone - Federal Unity Schools

30. FGC (mixed), Ikot-Ekpene in Akwa-Ibom State
31. FGGC (mixed) Ikot-Obio-Itong in Akwa-Ibom State
32. FSTC (mixed), Uyo in Akwa-Ibom State
33. FGC (mixed), Ikom in Cross-River State
34. FGGC Calabar in Cross-River State
35. FGC (mixed) Warri in Delta-State
36. FGGC Ibusa in Delta-State
37. FGC (mixed) Ibillo in Edo-State
38. FGGC Benin in Edo-State
39. FSTC (mixed) Uromi in Edo-State

40. FGC (mixed) Port-Harcourt in Rivers-State
41. FGGC Abuloma in Rivers-State
42. FSTC mixed) Ahoada in Rivers-State
43. FGC (mixed) Odi in Bayelsa-State
44. FGGC Imiringi in Bayelsa-State
45. FSTC (mixed), Tungbo in Bayelsa-State

North Central Zone - Federal Unity Schools

46. FGC (mixed), Vandeikya in Benue-State
47. FGGC Gboko in Benue-State
48. FGC Otobi in Benue-State
49. FSTC (mixed), Otukpo in Benue-State
50. FGC (mixed), Ugwolawo in Kogi-State
51. FGGC Kabba in Kogi-State
52. FSTC (mixed), Ogugu in Kogi-State
53. FGC Ilorin in Kwara-State
54. FGGC Omu-Aran in Kwara-State
55. FGC (mixed) Minna in Niger-State
56. FGGC Bida in Niger-State
57. FGC (mixed), New-Bussa in Niger-State
58. FSTC (mixed), Shiroro in Niger-State
59. FGC (mixed), Jos in Plateau-State
60. FGGC Langtang in Plateau-State
61. FGC (mixed) Kwali in Federal Capital Territory
62. FGGC Bwari in Federal Capital Territory
63. FGGC Abaji in Federal Capital Territory
64. FGBC (boys only), Garki in Federal Capital Territory
65. FGC (mixed), Rubochi
66. FSTC (mixed) Orozo in Federal Capital Territory
67. FGC (mixed), Keffi in Nasarawa-State
68. FGGC Keana in Nasarawa-State
69. FSTC (mixed), Doma in Nasarawa-State

South West Zone - Federal Unity Schools

70. King's College (boys only), Lagos-Island in Lagos-State
71. FGC (mixed), Lagos

113

72. Queen's College, Yaba in Lagos-State
73. FSTC (mixed), Yaba in Lagos-State
74. FGC (mixed), Odogbolu in Ogun-State
75. FGGC Shagamu in Ogun-State
76. FSTC (mixed), Ijebu-Mushin in Ogun-State
77. FGC (mixed), Idoani in Ondo-State
78. FGGC Akure in Ondo-State
79. FSTC (mixed), Ikare-Akoko in Ondo-State
80. FGC (mixed), Ikirun in Osun-State
81. FGGC Ipetumodu in Osun-State
82. FSTC (mixed), Ilesa in Osun-State
83. FGC (mixed), Ogbomoso in Oyo-State
84. FGGC Oyo in Oyo-State
85. FSTC (mixed), Igangan in Oyo-State
86. FGC (mixed) Ikole-Ekiti in Ekiti-State
87. FGGC Efon-Alaye in Ekiti-State
88. FSTC (mixed), Usi-Ekiti in Ekiti-State

North West Zone - Federal Unity Schools

89. FGC (mixed), Kiyawa in Jigawa-State
90. FGGC Kazaure in Jigawa-State
91. FSTC (mixed) Mallam Madori-Birniwa in Jigawa-State
92. FGC (mixed), Kaduna in Kaduna-State
93. FGGC Zaria in Kaduna-State
94. FSTC (mixed) Kafanchan in Kaduna-State
95. FGC (mixed), Kano in Kano-State
96. FGGC Min-Jibir in Kano-State
97. FSTC (mixed), Ganduje in Kano-State
98. FGC (mixed), Daura in Katsina-State
99. FGGC Bakori in Katsina-State
100. FSTC (mixed), Dayi in Katsina-State
101. FGC (mixed), Birnin-Yauri in Kebbi-State
102. FGGC (mixed) Gwandu in Kebbi-State
103. FSTC (mixed) Zuru in Kebbi-State
104. FGC (mixed), Sokoto in Sokoto-State

105.   FGGC Tambuwal in Sokoto-State
106.   FGGC Gusau in Zamfara-State
107.   FGC (mixed), Anka in Zamfara-State

In the past, essentially before 1980s, private schools that were not set up by missionary institutions were never popular choices of parents for their children and wards. The secondary schools of first choice were the government schools and the frontline various religion missions in Nigeria. Consequent to the broken-down standard and depletion of basic infrastructures that made the old generation heritage schools attractive, private individuals invested in the setup of private secondary schools in Nigeria. Some of them constitute the best secondary schools in Nigeria of today. The only snag is that the majority of the good ones among them are for the rich, not many working-class people can afford the schools. Some of the premium private secondary schools in Nigeria include: Oladele Olashore International School, Iloko in Osun-State, it was established in 1994; Adesoye College, Offa in Kwara-State; American International School of Lagos; Grange High School, Lagos, British International School, Lagos, it was established in September 2001; American International School, Abuja, it was established on 1993; Lekki British International High School, it was established over two decades ago; Day Waterman College, located along the Abeokuta-Sagamu expressway in Ogun State and it was established by Tayo Aderinnokun; Greenspring School, Lagos; Meadow Hall Schools, Lekki, Lagos, Loyola Jesuit School, Abuja, Hill Crest School, Jos; Corona Secondary School, Agbara in Ogun State; Atlantic Hall, Epe in Lagos; Chrisland College High School, Ikeja; Dowen College, Lekki Lagos; Whiteplans British School, Abuja; International Community School, Abuja; Greenoak International College, Port Harcourt; Greenoak International School is located around the GRA Phase 3 directly Tombia Road extension in Port Harcourt; Norwegia International School, Port Harcourt and Nigerian Turkish International College, Abuja

SECTION TWO

THE GRAMMAR SCHOOL

CHAPTER NINE

THE GRAMMAR SCHOOL

Nigeria, being a British colony, the secondary education was expectedly structured to a large extent along the British system right from colonial days. The grammar schools traditionally are government secondary schools that select their pupils by means of an examination taken by children at age 11, usually known as the 11+. Under the grammar school system in the United Kingdom where grammar schools have existed since the 16th century, students who pass the central examination are given admission to the local grammar school, while those who do not can go to the local secondary modern school which had since been phased out in Nigeria or a comprehensive school, in which pupils of all abilities and aptitudes are taught together. Nigerian system over the years is not different from this, in the government schools, but there has been no consistency in its effective management.

Structurally, the secondary education was packaged such that the grammar schools will focus on academic studies, with the assumption that many of their pupils would go on to higher education while the comprehensive schools were intended for children who would be going into trades. Also, technical colleges were introduced. Essentially, the system has kind of divided the students to the categories of those destined for university and better jobs, and those deemed more suitable for less celebrated professions. During the 1950s and 1960s in the UK, it was said by the Labour politicians and egalitarian educationalists, that the selective education system was reinforcing class division and middle-class privilege. Consequently, in 1965, the government ordered local education authorities to start phasing out grammar schools and secondary moderns, and replace them with a comprehensive system. This reminds me of a story. An older cousin told me about his experience with a modern school admission in the 1960s. His half-brother got admission into Ifaki Grammar School, while he gained admission into Methodist Modern School, Ifaki. He was happy initially, but when his brother told him that if he was not convinced that grammar school was higher than his modern school, they should put their books in pyramidal form beside one another. My cousin revolted when his brother's books were more. It took the intervention of my father to see that he joined the grammar school in the following session for him to be happy. The Nigerian education system has been running riotous during unstable governments and inconsistencies of government policies over the years. At some point, government took-over private schools only to return them to owners after running them aground.

9.1. **Ifaki Grammar School Heritage: An Overview of 1957-2021**

Up till the early 1950s, there was only one secondary school in the old Ekiti Province, Christ's School, Ado-Ekiti and it was established by the missionaries. Efforts of some early educated Ekiti indigenes in the Diaspora led to the establishment of Ekiti Parapo College, Ido-Ekiti in 1954. This development spurred other communities to start considering having a secondary school in their domain. The regional government of the day, under the leadership of Chief Obafemi Awolowo helped the situation by offering to take-over the responsibility of schools from the communities that were able to provide basic infrastructure up to a specific level. Ifaki community was encouraged by this favourable government policy among other reasons to establish their own secondary school.

In 1955, the idea of having a secondary school was muted by the community leaders, the enlightened sons and daughters of Ifaki-Ekiti. The first formal meeting on the plan of the community to establish Ifaki Grammar School (IGS) was held on December 28th 1955. At the first executive meeting of the committee for the establishment of IGS, Chief D. O. Adetunmbi was appointed the treasurer for the Grammar School fund on April 21st 1956. IGS was approved by the government in Ibadan on August 24th 1956. The first bush clearing on the IGS permanent site, by the town people and students was done on March 19th 1957. The Grammar School, Ifaki-Ekiti started with 28 boys on April 21st 1957. The two pioneer teachers were Chief J. O Adeoya (Principal) and Chief D. O. A. Adetunmbi (Senior Tutor). They worked and served meritoriously for over 15 and 18 years respectively.

The Ifaki Progressive Union championed the communal effort on the grammar school project, which eventually led to the establishment of the community secondary school in January 1957. The school started initially within the town in Ilogbe quarter and later moved to its permanent site on Ado-Ekiti road. While academic work was in progress in the temporary site, efforts were made to clear the permanent site. On the 10th of March 1957, the community went for the first time to clear the school site. The following day the students went with Chief D.O. Adetunmbi to uproot trees and clear the site while the town people went to the site on the 19th of March 1957.

Sitting L-R: x, Vincent Ojo IV, Jacob Adegboyo, Gabriel Oguntuase, the vacation Jobber from UI, Joseph Ogunleye, Isaac Ariyo, & Olu Omotayo.

Standing 1st Row L-R: Borode Rufus, Adedayo Ojo II, Diya Ogungbamigbe, Adeyemi Falore, Joseph Ajayi I, Ademola Adesina, Femi Ayodele, Michael Ojo III, Dele Omole, Gbadamosi Dada I, Bisi Adebunmi, Ebenezer Babatope, Biodun Agbelese, Dada Ogundipe, Oladele Ajala, Danson Asubiojo. Standing 2nd Row L-R: Remigius Fagboyo, Alade Adeosun, Jonathan Odeyale, Femi Fadiya, Andrew Adewumi, Chief D.O. Adetunmbi (author), Adebayo Ojo I, Bisi Aladegbami, Adegboyega Omodele and Joseph Omodayo

The school formally opened at the new site with Messrs Adeoya, Adetunmbi and Oni on the 23rd of January 1958. To ensure and facilitate regular morning devotion in the school, Chief Adetunmbi moved his 1916 model pedal organ, on the 17th of February 1958 to the school ground for use during assembly devotions in the school, temporarily. The school was officially opened by Mr. J. O. Oye, the Permanent Secretary to the Ministry of Education in the old Western Region, on the 1st of March 1958 at 11:00 a.m. Chief J. O. Ojo, the then Principal of Wesley College, Ibadan was honoured with Eletolua chieftaincy title on this memorable day by His Royal Majesty, Oba Olojido Olayisade in recognition of all his efforts on the IGS project. A general thanksgiving service for the school was held on the 2nd of March 1958 and a total of four pounds, fifteen shillings and seven and half pence was collected as offerings during the service.

Chief J. O. Adeoya was the first Principal of Ifaki Grammar School. He was a product of Wesley College, Ibadan in 1944, holder of Bachelor of Arts degree from the University College, Ibadan in 1952 and attended University of London for his post graduate course in Education. He was in charge of the school for over fifteen years, January 1957 to December 1972. The Methodist Mission contributed tremendously to the running of IGS in its early years. The first set of students graduated in December 1962 and 16 out of 17 candidates who sat for the school certificate examination passed.

Sitting, Chief J. O. Adeoya (4th from right) and Chief Adetunmbi (4th from left) with the first set of students in 1957

On the 5th of June 1958, a re-conditioned organ was bought for the school for 76 pounds, 7 shillings and 10 pence. A total sum of 83 pounds was spent, cost and freight inclusive. Mr. Osunkunle arrived from the University College, Ibadan on the 11th of June 1959 and assumed duty as the second graduate teacher in the school. The early teachers worked conscientiously for the school. The founding principal was an all-rounder, He taught Latin, English and Mathematics and was on duty every day throughout the week. Also, while Chief Adetunmbi was an active class teacher, he was doing other administrative jobs. At a point in time he was the housemaster, games master, bursar and the admission officer. His students also recalled that Baba as Chief Adetunmbi was popularly called taught them all subjects including those without class teachers. He was quoted at an instance "We are all reading together, try and follow; I myself I am reading for the first time".

Members of staff of IGS in the late 1960s; sitting L-R: were Mr &Mrs Zachariah, Chief Odu, Mr Stephe, Chief Adeoya (Principal), Baba, Mr & Mrs Dudley Pickson, Mrs Catherine Agbelese, Chief G.O. Dada. Standing from left were Dr Segun Dada, Chief J. A. Fadare, Mr Dayo Ojo, Mr Abiodun Agbelese, Mr Bankole & the Bursar

The Board of Governors of Ifaki Grammar School appointed Chief D.O. Adetunmbi as the Senior Tutor on July 16th 1960, in recognition of his contributions to the progress of the school. Preparation for the final year examination of the first set of Ifaki Grammar School was in progress when the formal approval letter from the West African Examination Council (WAEC) was received on the 1st of April 1962. Three days after this cheering news, the roof of the school main block was blown off by tornado. A thanksgiving service was held on the 8th of April 1960 for the good news from WAEC and for the fact that nobody got hurt as a result of the tornado incident. On October 10th 1960, Mr & Mrs Siddigi and Mr. Lovine, the new expatriate teachers for the school were met at Ibadan by Chief Adetunmbi. Mr & Mrs Pickson arrived on the 26th of April 1962 to take up appointment with the school.

Mr P. O. Adewole from Imade College Owo succeeded Chief Adeoya in 1973, one year after, Chief R. A. Fayose, a native of Iyin-Ekiti served as the School principal in 1975 and was succeeded by Mr J. A. Alabi who came from Ekiti Parapo College, Ido-Ekiti and was in charge in 1976 to 1977. Chief O. O. Adebiyi was the principal in 1977 to 1980, Chief O. Faleye in 1980 to 1983, Chief E. O. Babalola in 1983 to 1986, Mr C.O. Agbele in 1986 to 1995, Pastor O.O. Adelugba in 1995 to 1998, Mr J.O. Olabode in 2010 to 2011, Mr C. A. Abe in 2011 to 2012, Mr R. T. Oso in 2012 to 2017, Mr M. K. Jegede 2017 to 2018 and Mr O. J. Omodara assumed duty as the school principal in 2018 till date.

Members of 1962-68 Set of IGS with Chief D.O. Adetunmbi in front of Geography Lab. Some members of this set include Dr Victor Olayisade, Prof Kunle Adelusi, Messrs Doyin Dada, Ajibade Fawole etc

The standard of the school started dropping when the school principals were not staying long (due to transfer/posting within a year or two) to sustain the lasting school traditions and culture of excellence entrenched by the founding fathers and dedicated teachers over the years. The dilapidated state of infrastructures that couldn't be fixed which was peculiar to most of the government schools in Nigeria did not help matters. The boys only school became a mixed school in September 1980 and in September 2018, it came back to Boys school only. The greatest setback the school suffered came when the campus was taken-over in 2008 by a newly established university in Ifaki and later annexed by Ekiti State University. This resulted to IGS students squatting at Methodist Girls High School, Ifaki-Ekiti from February 2009 to 2018.

Naturally, majority of the old students never liked the idea of the school premises that was taken-over. As a matter of fact, at a stage, some of us called for cohabitation of the university college and IGS so that our students would have access to the sports' fields and the alumni will still have some measure of attachment to their alma mater to facilitate more financial support for the progress of the school. Due to lack of consensus caused by the non-inclination of those behind the takeover of the school premises, the best decision could not be taken for the school for the benefit of the current students. However, through the intervention of the alumni body, conscious effort was made to relocate the students to the provided new site within the expansive land acquired for the defunct university, some hundred meters away from the IGS original premises. The financial support of the alumni association and few Ifaki indigenes is commendable, especially High Chief Eyemuju Bolanle Owolabi who donated a classroom block. All the concerted efforts and collective determination made it possible to make some building structures available for the use of the students in addition to the basic building the state government provided. The students resumed schools in the new premises in September 2018. A lot is still required to bring the school up to the required standard.

Apparently, hope is not lost on the restoration of the IGS heritage because some members of the old students are not giving up because of their passion for their alma mater this is why call for restoration keeps recurring in the forum of the global alumni body and at some sets' levels. In spite of the challenges, the school has produced many distinguished and successful men of various professional callings. To the glory of God, among the IGS alumni community are professors, royal fathers, federal ministers, a senator of the Federal Republic of Nigeria, judges, top military officers, many professional bankers, numerous high-ranking technocrats etc. It is our hope that things will look up for the school in earnest to measure up again to the standard of the cherished IGS when it was at its peak that parents sent their children from Lagos, Ibadan and other parts of Nigeria to come for their secondary school education in Ifaki-Ekiti. Up Ifaki Grams, up IGS, up School!!!

9.2. Ifaki Grams Culture, Traditions And Integrated Reminisces

Ifaki Grammar School (IGS) means a lot to people in different ways depending the relationship of each person to the school. The Ifaki community people that founded the school do have their stories to tell. The students from the neighbouring towns and villages that didn't have secondary schools in their community to attend considered it a privilege to attend IGS. Those non-academic staff and teachers and their children of course often have their sentimental attachment to the school for various reasons. In general, most old students have sentimental attachments to their alma mater, IGS alumni are no exceptions.

Personally, my fondness of Ifaki Grammar School as an institution and as a unique school premises are in many parts. First and foremost, my father was one of the founding fathers of the school, who spent 18 years of his career as a teacher and a remarkable school administrator developing the school. He was called upon by Ifaki community, from Ekiti Parapo College where he was planning to further his education to come and co-start IGS, it was a sacrifice he made. Secondly, I was born in 1962 when my parents were living in the school premises and had my toddling years with Dayo Pickson whose parents were the next-door neighbor white British expatriates. Mr & Mrs Dudley Pickson named their first child after Mr Adedayo Ojo, the first Senior Prefect of Ifaki Grams. Thirdly, I was a student of IGS from September 1973 to June 1978 from Form I1 to Form V. Fourthly, I knew most of the senior students that ordinarily I didn't meet in school by virtue of my unhindered access to the school premises and witnessing of various school events and ceremonies from late 1960s to early 1970s. Fifthly, Every Sunday, we worshipped together with some of the students at St. Michael's Anglican Church, Ifaki and Lastly, I saw students' procession to annual carol service at Methodist Church, Ilogbe. I particularly witnessed the loud shout of Waaahhhh when Chief Adeoya drove pass the procession in his Black Opel and *Baba* Jack when my father passed through them in his Peugeot 403 car with the plate number WL6703. I was also called *omo Baba* by the students when they saw me.

The students and teachers in 1970

Contemporarily, what constituted the heritage of Ifaki Grams that endeared the school to all ranks of stakeholders are entrenched in how the school evolved, the structure of the school compound with an effective boarding system built on Christian foundation, good curricula delivered by dedicated teachers, the **H**-shape layout of the school premises with an expansive and well-maintained fields for wide range of sports, the school dormitories – Alarada (Red) House, IPU (Yellow) House, Jones (Blue) House and School (Green) House, inter-House and inter-schools sports, dining hall experience, socials - welcome party for new students, among other reasons. A typical day started with devotion and prayers in the hostel by singing from Ancient and Modern, this will be continued at the Assembly Hall when the Day-students would participate. We had break at 11:00am during classes when interested students had the chance of eating rice and dodo from food vendor from town, *Mama pupa*, Mrs Omotayo was the favorite of most students in my time in the school. Siesta of one hour followed suit after launch, evening sports and prep after dinner. The day ended with devotional hymns and prayer just before light-out at 10 pm. The lasting school culture and tradition helped most students to be able to sing the first and the last stanzas of some hymns from the Ancient and Modern or Songs of Praise hymn books. In order for day students to get a feel of the full school culture and it was compulsory that Year 4 and 5 students should be in the boarding house. This will enable them to study more within the school premises for the final year examinations.

125

The school staff and the final year students in 1970

Fond memories of dedicated school principals and resourceful school teachers also endeared students to Ifaki Grammar School. My principal in Form 1 was Mr P. O. Adewole who came from Imade College. He was a man of distinct personality who spoke Queen's English and his first born, Adekanmi Adewole was my classmate, we were the youngest in the class, we sat next to each other we were best friends and the relationship remains till date.

I have very fond memories of Chief R.A. Fayose, a native of Iyin-Ekiti, in his immaculate white conductor, his signature official dress to school. He made out time to take us some literature classes in Form III. Likewise, Chief J. O. Alabi who was noted for speeding with his Peugeot 403 car, he got the nickname of opaque from students because he made himself as an example of an opaque body when he was teaching the students Physics. We were also blessed with some outstandingly resourceful teachers, some of them took us more than one subject in the junior classes e.g. my father, Chief D.O. Adetunmbi took us Geography, Bible Knowledge and Yoruba. The Map Reading Baba thought us in Form 1 was so rich to the extent that I found it useful in HSC and in my undergraduate days. Chief Akinyele was a brilliant geography teacher, likewise Reverend Ala who was a chemistry teacher and our music instructor. Chief J. B. Adetola, the vice-principal was in a class of his own as a veteran geography teacher. Other unforgettable teachers were Chief Kayode Ige who taught history, Chief Adeolu taught history, Chief Falana taught French, Mr Adegboyo taught Literature, Chief Ajibola taught Agriculture, Mr Orimoloye taught French with his HSC.

126

Mr Patrick Olorunfemi Adewole, the School Principal in 1973

The Successive Principals

Chief J. O. Adeoya   Mr Patrick O. Adewole   Hon. Richard Akinola Fayose

127

Chief John O. Alabi, Principal in 1976

Chief O. O. Adebiyi, Principal in 1977

Chief Babalola

Mr. C.O. Agbele

Pastor O. O. Adelugba

Mr. S. O. Longe

Mrs E. E. Bamisaiye

Mr. G. A. Adebayo

Mrs K. Ayeni

Mr. I. O. Olabode

Mr Chris Abe

128

Mr. R. Tolu Oso   Mr M. K. Jegede   Mr Remi Omodara

Past Teachers

Chief D. O. Adetunmbi   Chief E. L. Osunkunle   Mr. Fawole   Chief G. O. Dada

Chief JBC Adetola   Chief Jacob O. Ajibola   Chief Akinyele   Rev Funso Ala   Chief E. Olukayode Ige

129

Some of the Distinguished Alumni of IGS

Chief Ebenezer Babatope

Prof Ademola Adesina

Jacob Adegboyo

Abiodun Agbelese

Mr Adedayo Ojo

Prof Olu Akute

Dr Abiodun Oyebola

Prof Eric Fayemi

Prof Wumi Ajaja

Ven Luyi Akinwande

Segun Dosumu   Chief Bamigbe Ibitoye

Taju K. Jinadu

130

Rev Kayode Omotayo

Pastor Segun Fayemi

Ambassador G. Omotayo

Prof Kunle Adelusi

Chief Esan Ogunleye

Prof Martins Olorunfemi

Oba Adewumi Fasiku

Senator Olu Adetunmbi

Justice Ilori Akintayo

Dr Folorunso Ajayi

HRH Tunji Olaiya

CP Yomi Oladimeji

131

IGS had a good outing in sports, especially in soccer, hockey, athletics and table-tennis. Chief G.O. Dada was the evergreen games master for the school for many years. Inter-house sports were always actions packed and would remain memorable in the history of the school. I was a member of the school football team and was the table-tennis captain which took me to Akure when I represented Ekiti West in the old Ondo-State sports competition. Our hockey team played at state level in the late 1970s. The rivalry of Ekiti Parapo College (EKPACO), Ido-Ekiti and Ifaki Grams in football was legendary. Christ's School Ado-Ekiti, EKPACO and Victory College had HSC students which put the schools at an advantage to attract sportsmen from other schools. This often make football matches between IGS and these school often very tasking and tension packed because our team was always making a remarkable outing.

Newly inaugurated school prefects for 1977/78 session with the school Principal, Chief Adebiyi and the Vice-Principal, Chief J.B. Adetola

Boys' Scout squad in 1977, L-R: Yomi Adebowale, Sunday Egone, Chris Fajembola, Dare Adebowale and Ade Ogunleye (Achebe)

Reunion meeting of IGS 1973-1978 set held in the premises of Engineer Dayo Adetunmbi of 1970-1974 set, on 24/6/17

Reunion with the School Principal, Pa P. O. Adewole (center) 43 years after encounter at IGS, L-R: Seye Adetunmbi, Engineer Bayo Ademilua, Israel Adu and Stephen Adesua of 1973-78 set at Ibadan in 2016

In academics, the school had produced so many brilliant scholars. We heard about those we didn't meet in school and we met some as seniors, classmates and juniors.

Consequently, I like to conclude this essay with the story of the prodigious Samuel Adekunle Ajaja, a product of IGS. He was a rare breed academically in the history of Ifaki community and Ifaki Grams. Adekunle Ajaja was born in Ifaki-Ekiti around 1948 by extremely humble and indigent parents. After attending Methodist Primary School, Ifaki under a free education programme, he could not even process admission into secondary school because his very poor parents could not afford to buy an admission form. In 1962 through the grace of God and some philanthropic support, he joined the 6th set of Ifaki Grammar School. He got double promotion to the 5th set of IGS in Class II. While the 4th set was the last to spend 6 years in the secondary school, the 5th set was the first to spend 5 years. Ajaja came first in their first term examination though he did not make 1st position in the second and third terms in Class II, but led their set thereafter in class III to the final class.

Six years was then the standard number of years scheduled for secondary school education, but Ajaja completed his in four years and passed out with distinction in 1965. In essence, he came in with the 6th set and graduated with the 4th set. His set was noted to be extremely brilliant in the history of Ifaki Grammar School. His other mates include Rev Kayode Omotayo, Pastor Segun Fayemi, Prof Olu Akute and Prof Eric Fayemi. He attended Christ's School, Ado-Ekiti briefly in 1966 for HSC. He gained admission into University of Ibadan and graduated in 1970 with B. Sc (Hons) Second Class Upper in Physics and it was noted that his aggregates narrowly missed 1st Class honours. He had wanted to study Nuclear Physics at postgraduate level, but for one reason or the other, it was not possible.

Nevertheless, as a result of his exemplary performance, he gained admission straight for his PhD programme in Cambridge University to Study Computer Science on scholarship. Unfortunately, poor Ajaja could not complete this phase of his academic pursuit because he was seriously indisposed and had to come back home from United Kingdom. Regrettably, he did not survive his ordeal and died in the early 1970s at UCH, Ibadan and was buried in Ibadan. Ifaki Community, his schoolmates, and Ifaki elites at home and abroad indeed mourned him when he stopped the race abruptly which left his poor aged mother in sorrow. To say that I was pained by his transition would amount to an understatement because I was very fond of him in my innocent years as a little boy in the late 1960s/early 1970s whenever I saw him because he liked me and played with me. Life is cruel when brilliant person like Kunle Ajaja is wasted at a prime age. Adekunle Ajaja was indeed a very brilliant student, uncommon genius in his lifetime and a great academic of all times with unparalleled credentials in his domain. The good thing is that there are many old students alive today who were also brilliant in school and have done well for themselves and the larger society in their chosen career to the glory of God.

Up School Ifaki Grams, Up school IGS!!!

SECTION III

CHAPTER TEN

REMINISCENCES OLD STUDENTS OF HERITAGE SCHOOLS

10. 1. Aquinas College, Akure

Sir Olubunmi Famosaya wrote: An Extract from his Autobiography
…My going to the boarding house in Aquinas College Akure to start secondary school was actually the very first time I was leaving the company of my parents….I was quite young when I gained admission into Aquinas College and had one of the smallest statures in the school.

Aquinas College Akure was very famous for its sporting prowess. It was equally good in academics and socials. In all my years in the school, we remained on top in the Grier/Powell athletics competition while in two consecutive years in 1970 and 1971; we won the Omitola's Cup (Principal's Cup) in the whole of the Western State. In 1970 we beat Baptist Boys' High School Abeokuta 2-1 in soccer match to win the trophy while in 1971, we beat Loyola College, Ibadan 1-0 to bring the trophy back to Akure and for the first time. That year, about seven of our players featured in the Western State Academicals, the regional football team.

In athletics, apart from the Grier/Powell competitions, we also took part in the Quadrangular Competition. This was a competition organized for four foremost Catholic Secondary Schools in the South West and Mid-west regions. The schools were St Gregory's College, Lagos; Loyola College, Ibadan; Aquinas College, Akure and Immaculate Conception College, Benin. Because of this level of involvement in sporting activities, students of the school were always self-motivated in trying their legs or hands in one sport or the other. Although I did not represent Aquinas College in any sport, there was no doubt that I had built for myself a background in sports that was to later in life launch me into big time competition. Indeed, in 1968, a student of

137

our school represented Nigeria in 400 meters and 4 x 400 meters' relay events at the Olympic Competition in Mexico. His name was Ajayi Akinkuotu, aka Ajasco. In the course of my sporting activities, I met different kinds of people from virtually of all parts of the country, parts of Africa and Europe. I learnt a little about the sociology and characteristic peculiarities of various people especially Nigerians.

10.2. Christ's School, Ado-Ekiti

Chief Fola Alade: An Extract from Autobiography

My school admission number was 935 and we were sixty students in Form 1 slotted into two arms A and B with 30 students each. Mr Z. B. Olokesusi was my teacher in Form 1A, while Mr Awodumila was teaching 1B. We had a mixed school with boys and girls in same class. We were also into four different Houses for our permanent sojourn for the six years of our life in the school, Babamboni (Red), Bishop (Blue), Dallimore (Green) and Harding (Yellow). Our school uniform, white baft shirt with school crest (on your chest-pocket), also had a small coloured patch on your right chest as your House-ID. Each house had a House Captain, and a designated Housemaster, with a two-bedroom annex built with each dormitory. The Founder, Archdeacon Henry Dallimore, was some kind of rare rebel of a British missionary, transferred from the famous St. Andrew's College, Oyo, to be Archdeacon over all CMS churches and Manager of all CMS schools in Ekiti-land, constituting the present Ekiti State. With Christian courage and his energetic supportive wife, after touring round Ekiti, he chose the natural green land with wonderful natural huge monolithic granite rocks surrounding, with a perennial stream and fresh springs. He decided to settle and live on top of the Agidimo hill in Ado as his base. Not an Architect or Engineer by education, but he was a rare combination of an architect/planner/surveyor/engineer/builder, all rolled in one.

He had incredible vision, concept and construction execution skills. As young students who had never heard of Architects or Engineers before then, the site and the sight of the school, so uniquely planted on lower grass level plains, where school cattle grazed, simply presented an alluring and overwhelming sight to behold. On the west of Ado - Ifaki road was an axial straight road with cultured flower edges, gently lining up from the residences on the lower plains, to the Chapel, Classrooms, Laboratories, Library and Girls' hostel. The Principal's lodge, in local stone masonry, perched beautifully on the top brow of the hills. As if planned and built by God, the road intricately curves and twists round rocks and hillsides to terminate at the car park and official hilltop residence of the CMS Archdeacon and Christ's School Principal. The 1929 house on the very top of Agidimo Hill still presents a most stunning aesthetic spectacle that continues to challenge any modem architects, engineers, surveyors, planners or builders of today. It is now the Bishop's Court for Ekiti diocese.

Reverend Dallimore chose the site, surveyed and planned the school. He then organized the breaking of Agidimo rocks for use for foundations and walls and then personally supervised all the construction by the original direct labour method, employing no single contractor. His method was based on self-reliance, hard work, integrity and above all, dignity of labour and he firmly entrenched all these values into all of us from the start. A boy in 1946 was dismissed for stealing one shilling from another student's box, as we hardly locked our boxes in their open racks. He tested and engaged the masons, carpenters, and artisans paying them himself on a weekly basis. In later years, we, his students were his builders as we all had to learn Carpentry, Masonry and Gardening on every Crafts-Day (Wednesday). I can recall that from 1946-49 our set (Form I to IV), participated in the building of the school chapel, new hostels, classrooms, new laboratories-and staff houses, all in granite stone masonry.

Our daily routine was time-bound and well-regulated with bell jingles or rings. Bell woke us up and out of bed at 6.00 am for ten minutes of family prayers led by the house captain. By 6.30 am, we must each do premises cleaning, in and around the hostel. Bigger ones would cut grass or till the school farms while some fetched water from the streams for teachers and prefects. By 7.30 am, another bell called us to go and bathe. Eight o'clock bell got us in for breakfast m the Dining Hall and by 8.30am, another bell sent us into the Chapel for prayers with all students and staff in attendance. The principal himself conducted the very orderly and solemn service to start the day. He made the school roll call class-by-class, after which we all marched up to the classrooms to good music by the school band, of which I was part from Form II. By 11.00 am, we had a 30minutes break for refreshment for those who had the money for it. By 3.00 pm, we all must take our siesta for one hour within which no one must walk around. If you broke any of these protocols, you could be *put on detention* and lose your free open-day which was every other Saturday for going into Ado town which we all used to look forward to. At 4.00 pm, the bell sent us' all into the fields for playing and/or practice of various sports. By 5.00 pm we all went to bathe to dress up for supper at 6.00 pm After our collective dinner we quietly walked up to the classroom for our night study lasting from 7.00 to 8.30pm, after which another bell collected us all in the chapel for vesper service, taken by weekly night duty master in rotation. We then got into our dormitories for the night prayers by the House Captain followed by a house roll call and by 9.30pm a final lights-out bell rang for all to be in bed till the morrow. No more moving around; it was all regimented.

The school produced the likes of Chief G. B. A. Akinyede, Prof Sam Aluko, Chief J. M. Akinola, Chief Adewumi etc. The pioneer set of school certificate graduates was those known as the *magnificent seven*. They were seven students taught and coached by Reverend Dallimore in his house and scored 100 per cent pass in the 1945 Cambridge School Certificate Examination. They were S. B. Aje, N. E. Ogundana, S. A. Bello, V.A. Adegoroye, J. Ogunkua, Hector Omoba and J. Aborigine. They all passed their examinations and that gave Christ's School its first big boost. The 1948 set got recognized as the official first set of Senior Cambridge School leavers. They included S. A. Agbabiaka, S. Awodigede, S. O. Asabia, Jide Olatawura, S. F. Olujongbe, C. B. Oguntonade, M. A. Ajomo, I. O. Adamolekun, S. A. Aje, J.O Fasan, F. A. Adeagbo, J. Ogunkorode, Olowolafe, and Miss Oyin Odesanmi.

The regimentation kept us on the right side of the school's rules, culture, norms and name. We kept to the honour and integrity of the school, even when we were on holidays or not in school uniform. We were that much disciplined. Above all, we were taught, *never to be arrogant but to be proud of our humble homes and of our great school.* One thing that greatly fascinated us students was the fact that students took real and active parts in the search, purchase and actual execution of the new projects. For instance, class-by-class on each crafts day, as Electrical artisans, we installed the power generating set with the poles and cables under the guide of the Electrical Contractors. We also, as apprentice tailors, sewed some of the new uniforms, while we, carpenters, built all our school beds and shelves in box-rooms in the new hostels as well as class lockers and table tennis boards.

My classmates produced majority of our *school-eleven* football team which included Bisi Adu (Captain) Adeleke, Oye, Osuntokun, Lawrence, Faloye, Adamolekun, Akinyemi, while Bisi and Osuntokun were the two champions in Table Tennis. Generally, our Form V class made the school popular winners in most. We all had that confident mindset that was implanted in us at school that *every man is the architect of his own fortune/ misfortune* and that one can only reap what he sowed. Some four mates made grade one; a few more were in grade two, while others made the pass grade. Not unexpected, Kayode Osuntokun led the class with 7As plus 2Cs, closely followed by Olu Longe, Bisi Adu, Bisi Lawrence, Ilori, Falope, etc.

I give it to Christ's School: Yes, I really do mean this, having no doubt in my mind of the privilege I had, attending Christ's School after my very lowly home upbringing in Aramoko. At Christ's School, we were very well trained. Talk of discipline, Christ's School had it all. Every student was subject to the authority and discipline of any student who was his senior. Because most of us were young and poor, students were disallowed from bringing fine flashy dresses, watches or such tempting items to school. All we did was to face our books, work hard and live a life of contentment. We hardly padlocked our boxes, yet we had no thieves. A clean, humble and great life we lived in our six years at Christ's School, Ado. It guided me in training my own children, most of who attended Federal Government Colleges. We were groomed with the virtues of humility, integrity, modesty and honesty. In school, with everyday chapel preaching and prayers we were never short of copious examples and precepts in Christian injunctions. I find these more beneficial in later life and living. If a Christ's School boy is arrogant, one should check his home and pedigree. I can tell you that it is not in our character to be arrogant. We were specifically taught *never to be arrogant but rather to be humbly proud of our home and our school.* We also took a lot of cue from our teachers. We were told by our British Principals in Christ's School that *there was no place for African time.* If you are late for five minutes; your punishment duration was of a relative function of the time for cutting grass. And our parents at home dared not even read it in our quarterly report sheets We were made to get our report sheets after every quarter properly done with the marks you scored per subject, the fees to pay, the date school resumed, etc. We would bring back to school that score card signed or thumb-printed by our parents. No chance of fooling or cheating our parents either, since fees payable and items to be supplied by the school, would be indicated on our report cards. It was indeed for these reasons I insisted that my children should all go to Christ's School. It was only my first born that had the privilege of Christ's School. My second child also was at Christ's School briefly. The best friend I ever had was met at Christ's School, Professor Kayode Osuntokun. We sat on the same two-seater bench throughout our six years in school. From Form I in 1946 up to his demise in October 1995.

Prof Adelola Adeloye wrote: An Extract from his book "My Secondary School Saga"

A memorable event was enacted at the school quadrangle. It was the "night of the dormitory market"...We were huddled into the centre of the quadrangle, fenced round by the gaggle of old boys who were having the thrill of their lives. The representatives of the four houses picked from the class the boys they wanted.... At the tail end of the event, as head counts were taken it was discovered that Dallimore House was two boys short of its complement of boarders. Joshua Pereao and myself went to Dallimore House. They said that Pereao and I looked alike in those days with no particular physical distinguishing features, certainly nothing to betray any hidden talent and in particular, any athletic potential. The outcome of the dormitory market evoked miscellaneous responses: delight for some, dejection and disappointment for a few, and resignation for most of us. I deposited my box in the box room, like other new boys, in the appropriate place in Dallimore House. The long day was ultimately capped with an evening devotion when the house sang a song which gave me much joy. Since my initial vespers in Dallimore House, that evening song remained one of my perennial favourite songs. *The day Thou gavest, Lord, is ended, The darkness falls at Thy behest; To Thee our morning hymns ascended, Thy praise shall sanctify our rest.*

My parents found it difficult to pay my school fees since I entered Christ's School in January 1947. Before then, Dallimore had set up a scholarship to be awarded every two years to the best boy or girl in the entrance examination. I missed out on that award in my year. When Mason took over in 1948, he specially studied the background of his students and their scholastic performance. On the basis of my excellent performance in the school exammination in the early years and my general behaviour he did what was unusual at the time, he recommended me for the award of full government scholarship to see me through in Christ's School.I had great difficulty in paying my school fees of £6 per year in 1947 in Form 1.When fees went up to £17 in 1948 and higher still in the following year, my problem was compounded. The situation evoked the humane nature of the character of our principal, Rev. Mason. Many boys were in similar dire straits like me. In some cases, the principal waived some unsettled fees and arranged for indigent boys to work for the school during holidays for the fees owing. In order to raise funds for running the school, the school fees were increased to £15 a year. To soften the financial blow the increased fees created for the poor Ekiti people, Dallimore at the same time conceived the concept of having full boarders and half boarders. The half boarders would only pay tuition fee and get their food from home. The latter group would pay £7.10s in 1947. When I entered Christ's School, there were no half boarders as envisaged by Dallimore. For the first time, Christ's School was a designated centre for The Cambridge Senior School Certificate Examination in December 1952. Archdeacon Vining was the Supervisor for the examination. There were four of us in Grade One; Adeloye with 5 distinctions, Olatunde 5 distinctions, Akeju 3 distinctions and Adesokan 3 distinctions. There were 6 boys in Grade Two and 10 in Grade 3.

The Prefects of the school in 1978 with Chief Agbebi, the schoolpricipal and some members of staff

Chief S.B. Falegan wrote: An Extract from his Autobiography

I was nicknamed *Gum* because of my severe catarrh, there was *Eku* (Abodunde), *Tuupu* (Vincent Faloye), *Jakoloba or Naughty Adams* (Jacob Adamolekun), *Aiyekooto* (Albert Fabunmi), *Olibobo-a masquerade* (Kola Aluko), *Igo/Focus* (Bishop Elijah Ogundana), *Quayin* (Oludipe), *QED* (Poju Balogun), *Eleyinkike* (Oluyede) and *Easy Odes* (Odesanmi) among several names. Our set, 1949-1954 was unique in the sense that it was the last set that spent six years in Christ's School. The immediate junior class to us, the 1950-54 set, was merged with us to sit for the West African School Certificate Examination in 1954. It thus became the pioneer class that started the five years instead of six.

The teacher-student relationship was very cordial without sacrificing discipline or respect. One teacher or the other was in charge of each dormitory. There were teachers on duty on a weekly basis for the chapel, for the dining hall, for night studies and so on. We watched and admired these teachers with awe, as they mingled and chatted amongst themselves without any obvious or serious misunderstanding, however inevitable.

The school's uniform was very unique. It was a feature of the school which we met and was also there when we left. The uniform comprised white shirts and blue shorts with

143

a school tie and a cap to match. The school cap carried the emblem or the crest of Christ's School, which is made up of a cross - (written in Greek- *CHI* and *RHO* - translated to mean *Christ)* and super-imposed with a crown at the top with the inscriptions: "Christus Victor" at the bottom on a navy blue background. It is significant for the victory of Christ whose name we bear. That is why the school prayer is significant for its structure and composition: *"Grant Oh Lord: that this school may be a Christian school, not in name only, but in deed and in truth; for the sake of Christ, whose name we bear."*

The school anthem, *"Christ is our Corner Stone"* was not the first that Christ's School had. In fact, it had gone through some generational changes starting from its birth and growth from being a central school for training Standards V and VI pupils from all over Ekiti in1933. The name "Christ's School" was given to the school on the 10th of September in 1936 by the then Governor of Nigeria, Sir Bernard Bourdilion when, on his visit to Province, he visited the school.

It was in Form IV that I became the post boy for the school. I had to go to the Post Office in the town everyday on the school bicycle to collect school letters and newspapers for the teachers. It was then I developed an interest in reading newspapers, which later influenced my choice of studies at Fourah Bay College, Freetown, Sierra Leone in 1956. I was one of the students flogged once by Canon L. D. Mason, who once invited me to his residence and gave me castor oil to clear my coated tongue. I forgot all my books in his house for two days; I searched for the books, which he kept. When he later called me to ask for my books, I did not own up to the true story for which he rightly flogged me. School discipline took three forms: gating, imposition and detention, which is the worst of all after caning by the principal. The "black book" form of punishment, which required expulsion, was rarely used, except once against a student that went to the principal's residence to steal in collusion with his cook-steward.

Things that Rev. Canon L. D. Mason did to his eternal memory included: the replacement of our bush lanterns with a mechanical generator to give us electric light for studies between 7pm and 9pm before 'light-out' for compulsory sleep; the building of new permanent dormitories of Dallimore, Harding, Babamboni and Bishop (Mason) Houses on the west-end of the school: character-building and sense of fair play, justice and love for students. I can recall his famous speech at the quadrangle "I *am reluctantly compelled"* to expel students reverberates, resonates and remains with students of that period. The second was the incident that involved a student from Igbara-Oke who was a rascal and always ran into trouble but who was brilliant, honest and sincere. The school authority had taken a decision not to expel him but to request that he leave the school in Form IV at the end of that year. The student played the lead role in the drama, *"She Stoops to Conquer"* which was staged at the Quadrangle a night before his leaving was to be announced. At the end of the play, rather than announce the decision to ask the student to leave the school, Rev. Canon Mason joyfully held the student's hand and said, "No, Christ's School is meant to reform bad students as long as they are not dishonest." The student was retained to complete his studies up to Form Six and he later rose to become Nigeria's ambassador in many foreign countries.

Leaving Christ's School at the end of one's schooling had its thrills, sentiments, emotions and memories. After the emotion-laden *welcoming* "initiation" for new students at the beginning of the school year with *"Oh What an Ass (You are) I am"* sung to the tune of the British National Anthem, leaving the school at the end of one's studies, was equally emotional. The corporate arrangement by the school authority was particularly impressive with all the students assembled in the Chapel for the valedictory service. At the end of the year, the Hymn, "Lord dismiss us with thy blessing" always featured.

Prof Mobolaji Aluko wrote on **The Qudrangle**:
Social gatherings (for plays (both by students and visiting troupes like Ogunde, Ogunmola and Duro Ladipo), debates and talk by alums and other distinguished guests as well as those many end-of-year parties by houses and school societies (otherwise called "proms" in the US for example!) were where Christ's School boys and girls honed their social skills and debating prowess...that is if you were not too shy. I remember 1968, when I was in Form Three, and Senior Niyi Osundare (an Amoye-HSC-arrivee who was my College Brother in Lower Six when I was in Form Two after Njoku had left) wrote the play for Dallimore House in ourInterhouse Drama competition. Dallimore lost narrowly to Bishop Housewho staged Androcles and the Lion by George Bernard Shaw...yes the sameShaw. Osundare wept bitterly and most in Dallimore joined him, because we thought that his originality should have given us an edge.

In debates, Ven. Ajayi, Principal of Ado Grammar School, was a popular debating proctor, along with Mr. Oloketuyi of Christ'sSchool. Again, Osundare once took the cake: in one debate in the Form Six block, he intervened with English words none of which was less than six letters. Ajayi looked at him and said, "Osundare, I think that you just swallowed a dictionary!" The whole theater erupted - and I have used that line ever since, tog reat effect. Now Prof Osundare has gone on to become one of the preeminent poets,

145

writers, critics and winner of innumerable world-class awards. If hegets a Nobel Prize, say that you read it from me first. I too had my English moment in Christ's School, this time with Mr.Oloketuyi in charge of the debate. The topic was "Is the Woman's Place in the Kitchen?" and there was to be a pro and con positions. I remember that Femi Oyebode and a Girls' Section lady were to be on one side (I don't remember which), and some other pair naturally on the other. Throughout the day, I had decided that I must speak at the debate from 2the floor - some people were allowed to from the floor - so I kept looking for a big word to use later that evening, hoping that I would be called. I plotted it carefully. Understand the following: at that time, I was in the habit of reading a dictionary like I read a book. I learnt it from my childhood friend Wande Ojehomon (he is currently a Nigerian Ambassador that has been in Turkey, Guinea Bissau, etc. I don't know his current posting) who was then attending Edo College Benin City. I once asked him what he was doing, as he was carefully yellow-lining words in the dictionary that he had never used before, and then going out soon afterwards to use them either in a sentence or to speak to someone. His philosophy was that words were not in the dictionary to be ignored - and I have imbibed that philosophy throughout my life.

Anyway, on this fateful debating day in 1969 (I think), when the actualdebate was over - but before the judges announced their results -contributions from the audience was asked for. I not only wanted to contribute, but I wanted to be the LAST before the judges made their winners' pronouncement. That tactic almost backfired because Mr.Oloketuyi almost did not call me, but for *frantic* calls from some friends surrounding me that "Aluko wants to speak, Aluko wants to speak! "Finally, Mr. Oloketuyi recognized me, and asked me to make my contribution. Clearing my throat, I began to use the word that I hadd is covered in the dictionary that day: "It is rather *atavistic*....."and I did not get past that word before the *whole* assembly *erupted* in"Ehhhhh....igi iwe!" It went on for a few seconds........and Mr.Oloketuyi waved and waved to ask to hear my "explosive contribution."After the noise subsided, I started again: "I consider it eminently *atavistic*..." and again the assembly erupted. Mr. Oloketuyi then asked me to use another word, otherwise he would have to move on without me, that the night was far spent....so, I said "It is rather unsophisticated for any person to think that a woman's place is *only* in the kitchen. Ishould know, because my mother is a great cook, but she has a full-time day job in which she excels."That was how I finished my contribution - to my greatest joy that I had achieved my English showmanship! I could have come out on either side ofthe debate....there is value in both positions.

146

Whenever there were debates in the Quadrangle, some teachers took it upon themselves to ensure that some girls and boys did not make off to the woods surrounding the amphitheater for nefarious purpose....Chief F. A. Daramola was particularly suspicious of every body and girl, and would carry around a torch, and when girls were going back to Girls Section, he would follow them slowly with his Beetle car lights on....We simply did not understand why he was so concerned about our episodiccoquetry....haba, these were not her daughters! The House parties and Society parties were the crowning social events of the year. Getting a girl to accept your invitation was a great event. Having a senior (from another house for example) invite your girl friend to his house party - and she accepting - called for frantic explanations. Of course, it never happened to me....but I lie on that one. It happened, and when I asked for explanation, she said they were cousins. How come I did not know all of this time..."bawo le se tan?...you are from Ado and he is from Ikole, for crying out loud!"It turned that they were telling the truth, but I swear that they did not know it at that time....the boy told me later that theywere indeed cousins through some circutious route, and I was relieved, rather late. Dancing too close to each other was also prone to draw unfavorable glances from some overzealous seniors (especially of the Scripture Union sect) and some teachers. Baba Adetola was particularly proneto interfere: "*Sun m'eyin, sun m'eyin, ma jo tight!*" - as he separated boy from girl on the dance floor. He felt that calipers were not the right tool to measure the distance between a girls breasts and the boys chest during a Christ's School dance. But if you succeeded in getting a tight dance with a "loved"one, the "calorie" flow was something to boast about later. In fact, there was a Senior girl who was famed for giving her "kilo calories" to young boys who chose to dance with her, as part of their initiation process. I can still see her smiling face close to mine. I am not kidding. Christ's School was not a monastery by any stretch of the imagination. And there you have it! *Bolaji Aluko* 1966-70 set HSC 1971 (Dallimore House)

On Christ's School and Others

Engineer **Soji Tinubu** wrote:

I must confess, I (and my father) have a lot of high regards and respect for EKPACO and Doherty Memorial. Those were the only two Ekiti schools that Dad allowed me to consider out of comeraderie (sp) with his two Christ's School friends who also were principals for those schools in 1962. I believe the oral interviews for those schools conflicted with my scheduled interview with Canon L. D. Mason, so, those two principals rearranged their schedules out of respect for the Canon and both of them were smart enough to know that

"EAF" already knew where Soji would go. The two principals still went ahead and scheduled interviews for me at some odd hours in their living room/office. To compensate, both of my immediate siblings (now deceased) attended EKPACO...My dad was one of those Ekiti indigenes who worked hard, from Lagos, to establish EKPACO. And the rest is history. At my tender age (61), I remain ever grateful to my father Prince Emmanuel A. Foluso Tinubu for making sure I attended his almer mater instead of some of those schools.... Another reason to shout Alleluyah to the Lord! Up School!!!! *Soji Tinubu*. Bishop/Mason House, 1964-68 set

Dr Abiodun Adu wrote:

In my book, there are only two schools in the A-list of secondary schools (call it 'the Rusell Group' or the 'Ivy League') in the Yoruba nation, Christ's School and King's College, Lagos. I am pretty sure GCI Ibadan, Igbobi College, St. Gregory College, Lagos, CMS Grammar School, Bariga, Lagos would find a comfortable home in the B-list. Schools such as Molusi, Oyemekun, Loyola will' definitely' make the C-list....I have no intention of upsetting anyone, not in my nature and that of any Christ's School alum!

Dr Abiodun Adu wrote: on **Prof Kayode Osuntokun** and The School:

I will be the happiest should my *oga* and mentor's name be immortalised.... Prof was the most brilliant neurologist to date that Africa produced. I should know! My association with Prof dates back to 1964. *Oga* Kayode was a close friend and classmate of my late brother----Prof Bisi Adu.The two I gather were the best in their set and used to interchange the first and second positions in exams throughout their years at the school. *Oga* Fasuyi and another brilliant surgeon (Prof Adeloye) were in that set. *Oga* Kayode used to holiday regularly with my brother in Unilag. I loved the ride in his beautiful citroen car anytime we had to take him along to visit *oga* Sam Asabia in his Ikoyi residence.

.......I owe my career in medicine to God, brother Bisi and oga Kayode in that order. I tell you why. I was one of the 13 in our set to be selected for the HSC. I was selected to read Chemistry, Botany And Zoology by Otura (Ogunlade). This was hardly the requisite combination to read medicine. Little did I know that Physics was a must. Soon after the HSC entrance exam, and as my luck would have it, brother Bisi came home (Ikere) to visit papa and on his way back to Lagos, branched at the school to see 'us' (the Adus) and Venerable Ogunlade who was a friend of his. Both discussed the combination and Otura felt I was so good in Botany and that I should stay with that combination which according to him will lead me to a 'good' career in agric or forestry! Even now I chuckle at the idea.

148

All brother advised was that I work hard and obtain good grades in WAEC. He felt that I did not have to go through the HSC route to the university.

When the WAEC results came out and 'armed' with 4As and 3Cs and 1P, brother took me to his friend for advice. *Oga* Kayode glanced at my results and said Biodun, you will do well reading medicine since 3 of my As were in Physics, Chemistry and Biology and that I should prepare for the prelim exam. I had to repeat english to convert my P to credit which I did in '64. I can not recount volumes of lecture notes and textbooks *oga* Kayode gave me. Bless him. His only disappointment about me was the fact that I did not follow him into neurology in my postgaduate studies. But knowing that I had a distinction in OBS & Gynae in my final year exams more than compensated for that. Even though, he was not a Gynaecologist, he put in a 'word' for me when he was on a sabbatical at Hammersmith Hospital and along with Late Prof Akingba (Who always described me as the 'apple' of his eyes) to get me to Kings College Hospital where I was the only 'black' face in our OBS & Gynae department then. I visited him at cambridge towards the end of his battle with prostate cancer. *Oga* Kayode was a gem of a man. He led the field of medicine in Ekiti - nothing can be more befitting than to immortalise his name. I for one will be over the moon. His contribution in the field of neurology is revered around the world. The reference he wrote for me to Kings occupies the pride of place in my achive. *Biodun Adu*, 1959-1963 Set

On Owhatanaamp

Prof **Bolaji Aluko** shares his first day and first week experience in the school:

I also remember very clearly my first few days in Christ's School – the first day started with a crisis or two. My cousin, Chris Ofuya (now deceased) was in Form Four, and had wangled an assignment to his own house Babamboni for me, so my luggage was moved to Babamboni and I was assigned a room. Within hours, Prefect Tunde Njoku had stormed in from Dallimore House, to re-assign me to his own postdcroom and make me his college brother in Dallimore Block 4B - the room that I lived in THROUGHOUT my five-and-a-half-year stay in Christ's School. Yes...I did not live in ANY other block that I remember than Block 4B. Maybe once in Block 4A, but never away from Block 4, the newest block in the school then, and the last one close to the famous "Cafe." After the first service of the school year that day, in the evening, I was subjected to grillings by seniors, who wanted to know what my realage was (there was an unfounded rumor that I was severly under-age), know about my professor-father, ask whether I could speak Yoruba...all kinds of silliness, I thought. But the funniest grilling on that first dday was about how fast I could run, because

I told them that I was an athlete. Well, one of the seniors told me that the fastest senior in Christ's School ran the 100yards in 5 minutes, and how long did I think that I could run it. Thinking that I would be modest, I sheepishly said in 7 minutes. Ehn, that fast, the Senior said? You must be the fastest new student in the school, he said. Could you demonstrate how fast by running from this spot to that spot over there? Instinctively, I started to run - and then checked myself. Why should I be running at night to prove a point? Where is their stop clock anyway? So I refused, and loudly protested that I do not obey orders that Idon't think are reasonable. That was the beginning of some of my problems with some of the seniors. You can disobey them, but when you give them reasons why you disobey - and do so in good English, especially the more traditionally Ekiti of the seniors, and they were many - it made them madder.

Later on in the week, all the new students were invited to listen to some academic-gown-clad severe-looking professors from the far-away country of Siam, who had been specially flown in to talk to us about our upcoming career in Christ's School. After their talk, they then also taught us a song, and asked all the students to line up, and have oneperson in front carry a placard.The song in Siamese language? Owhatana ....Siam; Owhatana.....Siam; Owhatatana, owhatana Owahatana.....Siam It was soon after you found that you were being made an ass of - all of these professors were sham, with one of them being Senior Oyebode (I think, but now a real professor) and another Tunde Njoku - and you were admitting it in song, with the boy in the placard carrying a picture of an ass that he or the other new students were not allowed to see.

After singing the song in the quadrangle, it was when you went back to sit down, that the BEATING of all of us asses began - and all new students ran for dear life: from the quandrangle, towards the chapel, headed for the tap behind Puttick's house and towards Dallimore Block 4B....near cafe. One was terrified....I ran for dear life and my 100-yards-in-7-minutes held up. It was that terror that was visited in my Form Five (1970) on a lady from Queen's School or so (her last name was Allen, and her nick name before then or since was Allenco) who had come to do HSC. A smaller version of Owhatana was also done on new HSC entrants...this time with their starting point at the Dining Hall, in broad daylight. This lady was *tall* and *thin* and *fast* on her feet, but when her beating began, she ran like a hare from the dining hall towards the chapel, towards Harding House, towards... Dallimore Block 4B, near "cafe," begging not to be caned at various stops along the way, only to resume her run when she saw that the beating would not stop despite her pleading. The whole school practically watched her strife that day. It was so bad that Ogunlade *banned*

Owhatana for first year and sixth form new students from that year onwards....And so a long tradition ended...to the best of my knowledge. A postscript: Even if you had a brother come in as a new student in Christ's School in those days, you dared not tell him what he would faceahead of time on Owhatana Day. Today, he would read about it on the Internet. In this day and edge of the Internet, the secret of Owhatana could not have been kept for so long. And there you have it. *Bolaji Aluko*

Chief S. B. Falegan wrote:
I feel sad that an entertaining tradition was cancelled! It was because your generation turned it into violence and allowed wickedness to accompany it. Please prepare to revive it at the next Homecoming of the alumni. I will be there to demonstrate the peaceful approach of our time/generation. It was by merely substituting and singing Oh what 'an ass I am with Oh what an ass you are after a quiz such as "What is white and black and read (pronounced 'red') all over". The answer which is ordinary 'newspaper' is not got right by the new students and we all shout at them Oh what an ass you are. *S. B. Falegan*, Dallimore House 1949-1954 Set

     Ayo Ipinmoye wrote: Prof. I can say with certainty that the tradition of O Whatanass" ran from 1974/75 and was finally rested in 1978/79 by Mr. S. O. Agbebi the then principal. I know because I was in Form 1 in 1974 and my hazy memory says it was on Sept 14, in 1974. It was the most perfectly executed coup against us the new entrants. Not a word leaked of the beautiful misery that was about to befall us. They did not even allow us eat our seven pieces of *dodo* for dinner, claiming we were about to gorge on a sumptuous dinner. Well, we had four more years of spreading the joy until September 1978. A lot has been written about the social gatherings but the joint socials were also cancelled in the early 1978. The girls confined for classes to the girls section. Morality went down the hill very fast from that point.

     Engineer **Ajibola Ogundipe** wrote: I was in the 1976/77 set that experienced it and we got to know that some of us were smuggled out of school and so did not share in what befell us and not a few of us felt cheated and let-down. I remember that my college brother specifically came to sit with me at my dining table to make sure I had my dinner assuring me that I would still have the appetite for the main celebration's sumptuous meal. Apparently, he couldn't bear to watch me go hungry all evening and still go through the ritual of Owhatana. He, however, never revealed the reality and I still respect him so much for that, in spite of our family relationship. One major event that I still remember was the moment when one of the "professors" asked if any of us knew the meaning of the word. Sensing that it could be the lucky question to win him a scholarship as were made to believe one of us sprang up to answer. The word sounds like "Oh what an a** I am", and my friend simply shouted "*ako ketekete*" meaning a male donkey. He lived with that name all through from1976 to 1981. I am also certain we didn't have it in my Form 5, i.e. 1981. I can't remember that we had it in 1980 either. *Ajibola Ogundipe,* 1976-1981 Set

Kunle Jinadu of 1973-1977 set recalled as follows:
"I do not think there can be any memorable experience greater than the "Oh What an Ass". The five weekdays preceding the Saturday night of the traditional welcome of fresh boys constituted a study in how to preserve tradition. Friends, siblings and seniors -including my college brother- who must have had a taste of what was in the offing for me, were stubborn thread in the web of an incredulous conspiracy. They offered me forks and knives in preparation for the waiting treat of sumptuous dinner. I, in return, promised to bring them surplus food and meat! To recall that I was totally fooled by those Professors from the faraway lands would be an understatement. For a long time, that night, I was very happy meeting with 'world renowned Professors'. Even, when I eventually discovered that there was no sumptuous dinner and that the Professors were in reality some of my seniors, the feeling was devoid of disappointment. I was unbelievably excited with a vow to have my pound of flesh the following year. From that very moment, I commenced a silent countdown to the arrival of the next set of Form One boys. I think this was the spirit that sustained the tradition.

On Detention, Imposition, Supension and Expulsion
Professor **Bolaji Aluko** wrote:
Imposition, detention, suspension and expulsion were the four categories of sanctions that Christ's School officialdom imposed on students for various infractions, from the sublime to the ridiculous. Only the Governing Body could approve expulsion; only the Principal could suspend but prefects and teachers could put you on imposition and detention, with the latter being approved by the Principal and all infractions read out to the entire school on Fridays at the weekly assembly. Imposition involved serving as a few hours work on campus, cutting grass, usually on a Saturday when everybody was out on Open Day. Supension meant you would visit your parents earlier than you thought. Expulsion....well, I don't really remember who was expelled while I was in Christ's School....Well, I decided

very early that I would never "enter" imposition or detention, or be suspended or be expelled, so I worked hard at being a good boy from day one, shunning all bad behavior. But it did not last long – may be six Fridays. Suddenly, I heard my name in Chapel "Imposition: Aluko Mobolaji: Talking in Chapel".

I could have been hit with a feather....and immediately started crying internally - and did so externally to my college brother Njoku. I was just about to ask who put me on Imposition when Prefect Imokhuome (Njoku's best friend) came around to say that he had done so. But why? Because he overheard me boast the week before that I would never enter impositionin Christ's School. But is that fair? He then asked me: Did you talk in Chapel or not? Anybody who says that he has never talked in Christ's School chapel out of turn is a liar. I could not say so, and that is where that conversation ended. It also gave me an inkling into the notion that if the authorities really want to get you, they can cook up something that you yourself might not be able to deny - like over-speeding, or taxes.... There were of course some Impositions that were always funny: "Gross insurbordination", "urinating all over campus", "ridiculing and mimicking a senior", ...There was one classmate of mine who was on imposition every week for"absence from chapel"; a devout Muslim that we called RSK, he was a fundamentalist who believed that he won't be caught dead in a Christian Chapel, so he took cutting grass every week while serving imposition as his divine duty to Allah.

What about my first of two detentions, the first by Mr. Fasan and the second by Mr. Bob Fagbemi. I remember the second one fairly clearly. Mr. Fagbemi was teaching us about bones of a chicken in Form Four, and he was pointing to a small part of small bone with his big finger. I then piped up from the middle of the class: "Sir, which part of the bone is really what you have just told us about? "He got angry for such impudence - he and Fasan were friends, and I suspect they both thought me to be smart-alecky - and he asked me to leave the classroom and stay outside in the grass for the rest of the class...which I did obediently. Class over, and all my classmates proceeding to the next class that we had, I thought that it would be proper for me to go to Mr. Fagbemi to tell him that my punishment -should it not be over? He got angry, and asked me to go and get the detention book....and that was how I entered into detention for "repeated gross insurbordination to a teacher".

Mr. Adetola was the Detention Master, and he could not believe that such a well-behaved student like myself was in detention. So rather than assign me to grass-cutting - which he feared might have killed me; as a school librarian, I conveniently avoided much compound work - he assigned me to go and work in the dining hall for one week, to cook food and clean up with the staff there. I first had to report to Mama Alade ("Mama Meti, "the Matron), and again she expressed surprise, and handed me over to an Igbo head cook *oga* James that we had then in Christ's School. I ended up not cooking anything, not cleaning much, just ate good food of Mama Meti throughout the week - but did not attend classes either, and certainly not Mr. Fagbemi's class. So I got fatter and taller during my detention....

My near suspension started later that same year (1969) on a Sunday and ended two Saturdays later. On this particular Sunday, food in the dining hall was atrocious, and so five of us: myself (otherwise known as "Sacramento"), Toyin Akomolafe ("Tosco;" we were constant items together throughout our Christ's School years), Funso Ani ("Humber", always well coiffed), Kunle Osuntokun ("Sosopela", whose maternal grandfather was Bishop Osanyin, Chair of Christ's School Governing Council), and Bayo Agbede (his father was on the throne in Igbara-Oke then) decided to go to "Cafe" to eat pounded yam.

In short we broke bounds.....But we were not caught out of bounds. As we were returning, Mr. F. A. Daramola was basking in the sun outside his Dallimore House housemaster's house, but his children spotted us while we all ran in to the latrine that could have shielded us from him. Not knowing that his children had spied on us, we came out one after the other, doing as if we had just gone to ease ourselves, where upon FAD called all of us out, and asked us to confess, and he would do nothing to us. Eagerly we did – where upon he reneged, saying that we all came from such privileged homes that the Principal needed to do something drastic about us.

He packed us off into his Beetle car, and took us to Principal Ogunlade's house instantly.....then to the Girls' section when he spotted the Principal's car way up there. He reported that he caught us outside campus - haa, we all exclaimed! Ogunlade asked him to take us to his house. This was about 4pm on Sunday. Otura did not return until about 10 pm, at which point he dismissed us, and asked us to return on Monday. Then on Tuesday.....then on Wednesday, where upon he handed each one of us a letter of suspension, asking our parents not to return us to school until they could assure us that we would not "repeatedly break bounds". I could not believe my eyes! Me suspended? How would I tell my parents? Up until that point, I had not even taken public transport to Ile-Ife all by myself before (my parents' always sent a car to pick me up) – so it was going to be an experience. Well, what to do? All five of us decided to go and eat in town (since we were temporarily free anyway) and plot our travel plans at Kunle Osuntokun's grandfather's house at the Bishop's Court......not knowing that Bishop Osanyin was at home. He asked us what we

154

were doing not in school, and we played the righteous confessors, telling him exactly how we came to be caught. He then said, "Okay, I will talk to Rufus.....he should punish you in school.....go back to school" – where upon he called Chief Rufus Ogunlade on the phone to let us back. We were aghast: we had just reported our Principal to the Bishop ....how would we explain that?

How could we survive his wrath? When he saw the Principal the next day, on Thursday, he simply looked at us, shook his head, asked us to all go and change into our khaki-khaki, and report to him at the Girls' Section. For the next 10 days, ladies and gentlemen, we dug and built the foundation and some walls of the Girls' compound sixth form block.....and when I see that block today, I can still see our sweat there! But we enjoyed our work there too, because the girls gave us food and we got quite some attention as they went to and came back from classes. Infact, on the very last day of our work, two Saturdays later...which we did not know, since the principal freed us without prior notice – the girls had gone to town to buy us special food, but we had to eschew it because there was a possibility that the principal would catch us again over-staying in the girls compound simply to eat!

So that is how five of us spent our near "suspension" - digging, filling and eating on the girls compound.... *A footnote*: When you are suspended in Christ's School, you are given a letter by hand to take to your parents. But another one is sent by mail to your parents at the same time, may be even earlier, just in case.....even though events had overtaken it, my own letter got to my parents, and they were waiting for me....and not seeing me two or three days afterwards, drove to Agidimo to find where I was indeed serving my"suspension".

Christ's School and Sports
The Soccer Heroes by **Bisi Olawole**, popularly called Sinbad

Great Alumni, Many thanks for the recap(s) of the beautiful golden years. Oyenuga was our goalkeeper in 1973/74, when we lost to Atakunmosa, he was a very good goalkeeper. Oyenuga was in form five that year, and he left in June 1974 and became the number one goalkeeper for Loyola College, Ibadan, the year we won the Principal cup (Oyenuga was there to retake his WAEC). As faith will have it, we met his new team (Loyola College) at the Quarter Finals, and when Christ's School scored the first goal of the five goals we trashed them, he was removed, and replaced with a Loyola boy and goalkeeper and we added four more goals after that, it was such a good outing for my humble self, (with 2 goals) Umoh and Pisco in terms of Goals. Who can ever forget the greatness of the true

Ekiti son, Coach Adewale, who saw "Diamonds in the rough" and worked on them to become the best Gems ever. All our dedicated sport masters, Mr. Ayo Agbebi, his senior and assistant, Mr. Aderibigbe (*Omo Jesu, Ayo o, Usanan udaa?*), were very passionate about the team's success. No one can forget the team's Grand Patron, Baba Idera, who became the overall god father and the "spiritual" coach.

I remember when the team was ready to travel to Ibadan for the quarter final match with Loyola, some HSC students conceal themselves in the paco bus, (behind second class), baba Idera started the engine and the "*para*" students thought they were on their way to Ibadan just like that, suddenly baba Idera came down and walked round the paco bus, telling all of the non footballers to come down "*in boile ninu motor mi, inboile, ole ni kete rin, in l'oju ti; i yo iru Olatunde ke e gbabolu gidi, e to abuo rin, ole ni a*" meaning, you should all come down from my motor, you are all thieves, and shameless, can you not see someone like Olatunde, a small boy, who is a good footballer (pisco), who is even not quite half of your sizes, all of you come down. All the footballers felt so sad for them, since we 'already started 'jisting' and singing with all of them, and looking forward to our usual fun filled trip.

The 1970 First Eleven at Liberty Stadium, Olaniyan, Bode Fatobi, Makinde twins, Bajomo, Oyenuga, Imoh, Richard Adeyemi, Filani, Ogini in track suit.

Coach Adewale brought the best out of all of us then simply for his leadership, dedication and sense of purpose. He showed us what leadership was all about. He will always get to the Agidimo football pitch at 5:00am, in his complete training outfit, "lap the field" with us, run up the Agidimo hill with big stones lifted high over our heads for muscle strength, (no training Gym. with weights in those days in Ekiti, we made use of what we had, big stones-Okuta). We were sometimes on that field for over three hours, playing soccer for endurance building, we became a total package, wonderful footballers, with good manners and love for each other. The coach will always select the first eleven based on skills and performance, no favouritism. We all had fun playing football in those days with so much passion for success. We had dedicated leaders, that gave their time, love, and money for the success of the team, and in return, the team gave back their best, which was enough to bring home the ultimate prize; The Principals'Cup.

If my memory is still fairly okay, below are the names to the Championship squad:
Team Mascot: Aluko Gbenga - (Coachito, Alusibago).
1. Olugbenga Olowoniyi - Goal Keeper (Micky Jargar)   2.   Babatunde Anthonio - World 2
3. Joseph Olaye - Dead Run (Iku nsare)   4. Atapa Ukana –World 4 (Atami Maafe)
5. Tanwa Oyebode - World 5 (Gbesun)   6. Umoh Essien -World 6 (Umoh mi Mafe loo)
7. Ogunmoroti Thomas – Director   8. Olugbenga Olatunde - O Pisco
9. Faleye Akanmu Sina – Lagado (Ayiri)   10. Falodun Olatunde - Saigonta Umgbeti
11. Arogundade Ayo - (Arooo T)   12. Ajayi Samuel - Batoto
13. Emem Esenam – Sename   14. Olawole Olabisi Sinbad
15. Kunle Jinadu – Lawee   16. Arije Opeyemi - Aristo

90% of Christ's School Alumni don't know my full name, most know me as Sinbad Bisi, or Sinbad Olabisi, some think I am Adewole Bisi. Hon. alumni, my full name is Olabisi Ademola Olawole, Olawole being my last name, and Sinbad my popular extra name given by my uncle when I came home for my first term holiday in 1971. My uncle was a friend to Batoto's big brother, they both went to Victory College, Ikare (one of the *sukuru pepepes* - one of those "something like-schools"). Bato heard the name Sinbad, and the rest is history.
Up School!!! *Olabisi Olawole* – Sinbad, Mason House 1971-76, HSC 1978-80

157

Professor Bolaji Aluko wrote:

Wonderful recall by Sinbad the Sailor! That I was present at Liberty Stadium when Christ's School won that Championship Cup was one of the highlights of my life. It was very emotional... my brother (now Senator Gbenga Aluko) was the mascot of the football team that year in Ibadan, performing some football tricks during the half-time or so.....he said that they were required not to sleep before midnight, and enter the field with their backs.... some kind of *"kurube"* activity which they did not all believe, but if you did not do it and they lost, you would be blamed. Even I would do it, with amusement on my face.... One side story.... the two "Calabar" boys on our team-Umoh Essien and Emem Esenam-were actually children of lecturers at the University of Ife, whose parents were my parents' friends, and said that their children must come to Christ's School because my father and I went to Christ's School. At that time too, my (next) younger brother Steve Femi (Aficonene) was also in Christ's School (he entered in 1969), and I think that my other younger brother Gbenga (Coachito, the team's mascot; there is a sister between Aficonene and Coachito) entered in 1972 or 1973. (He completed his secondary school though at Fed. Govt. College, Ilorin) Gbenga is a great soccer player himself and was once called to Nigerian Eagles camp. So when his daughter now plays for England and New Jersey professional club, and his son Sone also once played for England - and now for Nigeria - and for Aberdeen (Scotland), they take after their father and uncle, not to talk of their grandfather (whose nickname in Christ's School was "Flamboro") Although I did not play soccer for Christ's School, I played hockey and tennis instead; my record as a legendary House competition football player is sealed forever. With a nickname of "Sacramento" and a Number 7 position, and fleet of foot, I scored freely and fast for Dallimore House in those days. *Bolaji Aluko*, Reminiscing

Sir **Olubunmi Famosaya** wrote:

I remember very clearly that the volley ball teams of Christ's School of 1974 and 1975 won in a resounding manner the western state school's Volleyball competition beating schools like Comprehensive High School Aiyetoro (Compro), BBHS Iwo, Government College Ibadan(GCI) etc after having sacked schools like Oyemekun, Ekiti Parapo, Ado Grams etc in humiliating circumstances at the local level. Then we had the likes of Femi Falano Femai, Segun Aganga a.k.a. *Eja* (onetime Federal Minister of Finance), Bunmi Famosaya a.k.a. Famoo, Nsien, Gbenga Oyebade a.k.a. *Asin*, Ossy Idemili, Jide Ogunjobi, Claude, Tokunbo Agbetuyi a.k.a. Jalus, Segun Alonge a.k.a. *Ewon* etc. That was then. The good old days when we conquered West in Volleyball and football that the old students were so proud that they donated a Coaster bus to the school. Today I look back 36 years after and am happy I was a part of those victorious volleyball teams. *Olu Famosaya* HSC 1974-75 Set

Segun Aganga wrote: An extract from the Foreword to THE SCHOOL, a compendium on Christ's School, Ado-Ekiti, by the author of this book
I consider it a privilege and a great honour to be a product of Christ's School, Ado-Ekiti. That, in many ways explains how delighted I was when called upon to write the foreword to this unique book on a great institution, Christ School Ado-Ekiti. I must commend Seye Adetunmbi for the initiative, his professionalism and the remarkable effort he has put into compiling this compendium on one of the best institutions in Nigeria.

Let me state here that from my personal experience, the training and the family values inculcated in us by our parents and those instilled in us by virtue of the school we attended during our character formation years, to a very large extent determine who and what we become in life. Yes, I may have been privileged to work for a top four Accountancy Firm and was a Managing Director at the number one investment bank in the world in the United Kingdom for more than 30 years. I have also served Nigeria, first as Minister of Finance and later as Minister of Industry, Trade and Investment, yet I would always credit my parents and Christ's School for laying the solid foundation on which others built on. In short, I am what I am today because I attended Christ's School, Ado-Ekiti and the family values I imbibed in my formative years.

A lot of the credit must go to my parents in particular my mother who insisted that regardless of the distance, I attend Christ School when I had the option of sitting for the entrance examination into Igbobi College and King's College in Lagos. To her, secondary school education should provide the very best in values-led education to young people focusing on three areas: Educational Excellence, Character Formation and Spiritual Insight. Based on her research, she was convinced that Christ School was in the best position to deliver these at the time. That was how my elder brother and I ended up at Christ's School. I also remember that she wrote to us regularly and every letter ended with two statements: "Always remember the home you have come from" and "All that glitters is no gold". On our birthdays, every child received a special present: a 12 to 15--page letter commending you on what you did well in the last year and advising you on what you could do differently or better. There is no way you could have passed through Christ's School in my generation and the sets before mine that you won't turnout well in future if you allowed the school values to pass through you. We were endowed with dedicated teachers who took pride in the success of their students after they left Christ School. Agidimo hills and the evergreen environs provided superb learning environment with very little or no distractions. Our day started as early as 6:00am with prayers. Within three weeks of admission into the school, you were expected to have learnt (memorised) the first and the last stanzas of at least 25 songs from the Ancient and Modern hymnbook. To tell a lie would certainly earn you a suspension while stating the truth after committing a serious offence may get you lighter punishment. Every year we went on excursion to different parts of the country to learn more about our fellow Nigerians and their culture. My first exposure to the eastern region was on such trips.

We were exposed to competition, drama and sports. I was in the school's volleyball team from form three. The team won the championship in the then Western Region and I was in the team that represented the western region at the first National Sports Festival. We also won a Silver or Bronze medal. In my fifth Form, I was the goalkeeper for the school football team. I was also in the school relay team, a triple and long jumper and I actively participated in the Drama, Literary, and Debating Society of the school. I also joined the choir (that was a directive from my mother) and eventually led the choir in my Sixth form.

Christ's School brought the best out of each child and prepared us to be versatile (all-rounder). We were groomed to excel in character and academics. Every Saturday, the Principal set aside an hour or two to lecture the students on how to prepare for the demands and challenges of "life/the world". It was not surprising that Christ's School students excelled in the universities they attended. It some point, a large number of professors in Nigeria were products of Christ's School

Unfortunately, the standard of education in Nigeria schools including Christ School has fallen due to a combination of factors. However, the formal handover of the school back to the Anglican Mission in Ekiti is a major step towards reversing the trend. The Governor must be commended for this. A lot of effort and bold steps would be required to turn things around. However, where there is a Will, there is always a Way. I have every confidence that before long the present and the future generation of students will be telling their stories as people of my generation have done in this historical documentary book. I sincerely hope that their "digital" stories will be much better than our "analog" stories!

The new improved Christ's School would require an academic programme that would be relevant to the economy under a robust governance structure that would drive the new curriculum for the school. The training of teachers, entrepreneurship and skills acquisition should be prioritised. As I said earlier, I would advocate for an educational system that will deliver Educational Excellence, Character Formation and Spiritual Insight. It was also appropriate for the mission to run schools alone in our time, but the reality today will require strategic collaboration with the alumni body.

Sir Olubunmi Famosaya wrote:
I didn't have problems settling down in school even though the environment was strange to me. I was coming to a school where boys and girls shared the same classrooms, the same sports arena, same theatre and in some cases the same assembly. Coming from the masculine background of a Catholic School, this amazed me but it soon became fun to me. There was this myth surrounding Christ's School. It was generally believed that once you were lucky enough to be admitted into Christ's School, your future was secured. Today, this seems apposite judging from the array of old students of this great school in positions of authorities across the globe. At a time in Ekiti State for instance, all the principal officers of government were old students of Christ's School beginning with the Governor, down to his deputy, to the Secretary to the state government, Head of Service and Chief of Staff. There were at least four Permanent Secretaries and several Commissioners and Special Advisers in the Cabinet.

I resumed class in the School in January 1973 as a fresh Higher School Certificate (HSC) science student who had just been admitted to undergo a course of study in PCB as we used to call it then. PCB then stood for Physics, Chemistry and Biology. As destiny would have it however, six months later, I made 360 degrees turn when I relocated to the Arts Class with a new course in History, Literature and Economics. This became a turning point in my life history. I had dreamt of becoming a medical doctor but Christ's School felt otherwise and showed me a new path which was later to become my destined path. I became so fascinated by my new course especially by the teaching prowess of teachers like Chief Oloketuyi and Baba Aluko of Ise that academics to me became as simple as play.

I recall that on a good day Baba Kigo as Chief Oloketuyi was then called would get to class and dish out the English stuff as if it was his mother tongue, "You are an imbecile", "I don't know what atmosphere must have tickled you into a foolish laughter", "You are fishing in the river of the devils", "You are sitting on a keg of gunpowder" "When disappointments come, they don't come in singles but in battalions" and so on and so forth. Such was the calibre of teachers that taught us in school. Acquiring knowledge to us was fun and so it was easy to assimilate. Many of us left Christ's School and gained admission into university that same year we graduated. Those who could not make direct entry made direct prelim. Direct prelim was a form of admission to the preliminary class (known as 100 level) without examination. But then, what was my first day in Christ's School like? I had just then come from Aquinas College, Akure; a school that was very famous for sports having then won the Western State Principal's Cup in two successive years. I was originally "shared" to Harding House but somehow, I ended up in Babamboni House, perhaps because my uncle, Bode Babayemi was the Housemaster or perhaps some of my childhood friends like Bunmi Obembe and a few others were in that House. Bunmi, who was an exceptionally brilliant student later retired as an Executive Director of Total Oil in Nigeria. I was on my bed early in the morning when a fierce-looking tall man pulled off my wrapper and shouted at me to get up.

He dragged me to the sports pitch and started reeling out his questions, what is your name? You must be new here. Which school did you come from? Ah! Aquinas? Then you must be able to do a sport. I was later to know that he was called Alagba by the students. His name was Mr Tunji Fagbemi. Alagba later changed his job and became the Director of Sports at the National Sports Commission. That fateful morning, he insisted that I should try some sports since the inter-house sports competition was approaching. I challenged the school's representatives in triple jump Gboyega Famewo of blessed memory and in long-jump, Segun Aganga who later became Minister of Trade and they were shocked at my first outing which apparently threatened their supremacy in the school. That was the discovery Alagba needed. I soon became one of the school's representatives in these events and by 1974; myself and Bola Akanbi from Ibadan Grammar School were already flying the Western State's colours in the triple jump event at national competitions. That was what Christ's School gave to me. On other occasions at future dates, I sparingly made the school's relay team at invitation relay races at the inter-house sports competitions of other schools.

During the football season, Alagba took me out to the football team but I was later cleverly deployed to the volley-ball team because a popular winger from a neighbouring school had also just been admitted to Christ's School. His name is Ayo Arogundade, who later became a Comptroller of Immigration. Ayo displaced me in soccer but gave me fame in volleyball. My first appearance on the volley ball court generated profound protest from the 'traditional' members of the team but other games masters in persons of Chief Aderibigbe popularly called O-Jesu and Mr Agbebi insisted that I should be given a chance. I was indeed given a chance and there and then, I was confirmed a regular member of the

162

first team and that same day, I featured in a match against Oyemekun Grammar School, Akure and on its grounds, we defeated their team. The news spread like wild fire that a new student called Famoo had surfaced as a volley ball potential. From that day, there was no looking back. That same year, I had my first call-up to the western state sports camp in preparation for the first national sports festival and by the following year, I had my first national call-up.

I recall with nostalgia one Principals' Cup semi-final match played at the Liberty Stadium in Ibadan between our school and Baptist Boys High School, Iwo. For one reason or the other, I had been ruled out of that match on the advice of Baba Idera, the then school's driver. Baba Idera was so influential that he could advise against the use of a particular player in a match. He did just that in my own case. When that match progressed and we were obviously losing, oga O-Jesu threw caution to the winds and insisted that I had to join the team. Even though we were down by 2-0, we managed to salvage that match and beat Iwo by 3-2. The following day I was excited to see my photographs on the pages of the Daily Sketch, a nationwide circulating tabloid then. We went on like that until 1975 when we won a double. We won the Western State Principals' Cups in both Volleyball and Football, a feat which won for us a Toyota coaster bus donated by old students in Ibadan to replace our wooden truck. By August of that year, not less than twelve Christ's School Students represented Western State at the National Sports Festival in football and volleyball in Lagos. Anytime we went to play, we prayed and sang and sang and prayed and we were never let down by that the great Redeemer whose name we bear.

And truly He remained our cornerstone that gave us hope, joy and grace to be what we are today. Up School!!!

10.3.   Ifaki Grammar School

Adedayo Ojo, the First Senior Prefect of the school wrote:

Ifaki Progressive Union under the leadership of Chief A. B. Omodele spearheaded the raising of the needed funds for the take-off and meeting of the necessary conditions for the establishment of secondary schools as laid down by the Regional Government. Ifaki Grammar school took off officially on 24th January 1957 in a building comprising four rooms and a hall. While the rooms served as our hostels, the hall accommodated our classroom for 33 students, side by side the dining room and common room for the indoor game of Table-Tennis. The boarders resumed on Saturday 22nd January, 1957 while I was the first and only day student who came in on Monday, January 24th. Apart from the main building that housed the classroom, the dining room and dormitories, there was a kitchen with a store adjoining it. We also had a makeshift bathroom and a pit latrine. A well was also available to supply us water. The space between the main building and the kitchen served as playground for the younger ones to play "toronto".

We had only two faculty members, namely the Principal, Chief Joseph Ojo Adeoya and his only assistant, Chief David Opeyemi Adetunmbi. While the Principal taught English Language, Literature in English, Latin and Geometry, Chief Adetunmbi taught Yoruba, History, Geography, Bible Knowledge, Arithmetic and Algebra. Chief Adetunmbi was also the Housemaster and his residence was next to the school building while the Principal was living in town. Looking back now, these two gentlemen, at the prime of their lives, to have left the comfort of plumb jobs and city life, to come and take on the pioneering tasks of a new secondary school in the heart of Ekiti land speaks volumes of their patriotism and selflessness. The Principal was a Housemaster and a teacher in Igbobi College, married to a Sierra Leonean lady. Leaving Lagos with all the facilities for Ifaki must have been a very difficult decision. On the other hand, our Housemaster had a good job as a teacher in Ekiti Parapo College, established earlier in 1954 in Ido Ekiti. They both answered the call to duty from their town of nativity. Chief Agunbiade was the cook all my days at IGS. He used to be at St. Gregory's College, Obalende, Lagos.

Our school uniform consisted of Pharaohs khaki short sleeved shirt and nicker, while our Sunday wear was made up of a white shirt on long trouser and a white coat on top. The standard pair of shoes permitted was a pair of brown sandals. Sucks were not compulsory but definitely there was no tie. The school fee was £25 for the first term and £14.10 shilling for each of the second and third terms. The fees took care of text books in the first term as well as tuition and boarding fees. In the dry season of 1957, that is in the third term, we had to be going to *Aragba* stream to go and fetch water. As the lamp monitor, I would carry the only Tilley lamp on my head, and stay in the middle of the queue of students late at night to fetch water.

Chief J. O. Adeoya

The Principal, one morning broke the news to us that if we would move to the new site the following year, we should be prepared to build an assembly hall and a football field while the Ifaki community would build for us the main block of 5 classrooms. With joy, the first set received the good news. The big boys were chosen as axe men, while the rest of us were carriers of axes, hoes and cutlasses. The axe men were those responsible for hewing the heavy logs of wood of the rain forest where the football field was finally located. The rest of us ended up clearing the bush to the limit of our strength. 3,000 mud blocks needed for building the Assembly/Dining hall were also moulded, rain or sunshine. Usually, we would leave for the new site immediately after lunch and come back for dinner and the evening prep.

Chief David Opeyemi Adetunmbi

The building of the first block of 5 classrooms was awarded to an Ibadan based contractor, at a cost of £3,000. The roof design of the structure turned out to be unique and for a long time after its erection, that first building remained a master piece throughout the then Western Region. By January, 1958, we resumed at the new site. The two classrooms nearest to the Principal's office accommodated forms one and two, while the remaining three rooms served as our dormitory. The bookstore on the extreme right-hand side of the building was our Housemaster's accommodation. This again signified the sacrifice Chief Adetunmbi had to make for the upbringing of the students at the expense of his personal and family comfort and convenience because his family was staying in town away from him. The official opening of the school took place on March 7th, 1958 by Mr J. O. Oye, the Parliamentary Secretary, Ministry of Education. It was a colourful ceremony and Chief Adetunmbi composed and taught us a special rendition, titled *"ohun rere ha le jade lati Nasareti wa"* (Can anything good come from Nazareth)?

165

By 1959, January, the hostels, Alarada House Jones House, IPU and School House had been built with teachers' quarters, and the dining hall. The physical development experienced was astronomical courtesy of the foresight and financial prudence of the Principal and his team. We had our subject recognition inspection for approval in 1960 but the school was not approved to present candidates for the WASCE. By 1961, the three laboratories were already in place. Expatriates to teach Physics and Chemistry were also on ground by 1962 namely Mr Dudley Picston for Chemistry and Mr. V. C. Jose, an India for Physics. Whereas the 1962 set could not offer any Science subject at the school certificate level, the 1963 set was able to offer Physics and by 1965, the two sets that merged together were already ripe to offer Chemistry and Physics and Biology. By 1960, the Lawn Tennis clay Court was already in use. Football was the main game and we had a formidable football team

The faculty members were very versatile. The Principal was able to teach us Geometry up to Form four, even though he was a graduate of History. He also taught us Latin until the arrival of Chief Layiwola Oshunkunle who took over the teaching of Latin and History from five. Of course, from Chief Adetunmbi, we first learnt that Biology was a combination of Botany and Zoology, though his specialty was in Geography, Bible Knowledge, Yoruba which subjects he taught us from forms one to six. He also taught Algebra and Arithmetic the first three years of our stay in the school. Prep was observed twice each day after the afternoon siesta and dinner. In the evening prep, the lamp monitor would put on the gas lamps and position one in each classroom. This was my major role from 1957 till 1961.

There was a lot of healthy rivalry amongst students. Exam time was serious time. Reading at night was not officially permitted but it was a common practice especially at the approach of terminal exams. Piccolo lamps with white shades would be placed in a box with a small hole made therein just to allow enough Ray of light fall on the page you were reading. The Housemasters must have been turning a blind eye on this night reading after lights out. Of course, lights out used to be observed religiously and enforced by the House Prefects. If you tried to greet your classmate when exam was approaching, you would be lucky to have a nod in response as if saying hello to you would cause a leakage of all that has been stored upstairs.

The school's motto then was in Latin but translated to mean "Marry Knowledge to Character"; while the School Magazine was "VERITAS", meaning truth. It was therefore not surprising that emphasis was placed on Christian virtues and values like diligence, hard

166

work, transparent, honesty, discipline and respect for others and constituted authorities. These are the attributes that have helped us as alumni/alumnae of this great school.

Venerable Luyi Akinwande wrote:

…When finally, God granted me open doors to be admitted to Ifaki Grammar School's form one in 1962, though three years later than it should have been, no-one could have been happier than I was. The choice of IGS was made even though I had been offered admission by Annunciation School and Amoye Grammar School, both in Ikere but I was unable to take up either offer for funding reasons. Despite the golden opportunity to start my secondary education in Ifaki Grammar School in 1962, my disappointment knew no bounds when later, what should have been the start of my second year in January 1963, I was only able to leave home with £2 out of the £30 school fees needed for the first term of the new year. … ..At the beginning of 1964, it was time to return to school but still the funds weren't there. The only saving grace I had was that the school was open to those willing to attend as day students. It was bad enough that I had lost a year and was therefore not in the same class with those I started with in 1962, but to become a day student was to add insult to injury. Although, there was a bright side in that I wouldn't be available to be punished by seniors (including my former mates) as a day student. With a few other students, we hired accommodation in the cross roads area of the town and thus began what eventually saved me from missing the secondary education which I cherished so much.

In those days, studying for and passing examinations were no big deals for me, thank God. But there was another incentive for me to be the best that I could be after I was hinted there was the prospect of being given a double promotion by the school if one did very well. But when that chance came, a teacher stood against me for reasons best known to him. In the end, I had no regrets. Although, a number of those who got double promotions went ahead to do well academically later, still in other cases, this ruined the educational careers of many others. Indeed, the fact that I later passed the G.C.E Ordinary Level Examination in six subjects at credit level at the end of my fourth form and without quitting the course was a consolation for the years I lost and spent away from schools.

I returned to School as a boarder for the third term of the 4th Class and also the final year. But a number of experiences in school are worthy of being documented here. I recollect we had an end of year party in class one when the table was specially decorated with white table cloth, plates, spoons, knives, tea cups and there were some cubes of sugar on the table. Not knowing what the cubes of sugar were intended for, I added same to my rice which ruined the dinner for me. Don't ask me how I managed using the cutlery. On another occasion, when there were no offers by people to represent the School House to which I belonged in running the 880 or so yards race the following morning, I offered myself to run but managed not to complete the race. Indeed, I have many reasons to thank God for taking me through IGS but chief among this is that hardly would I have been able to successfully go through secondary school but for the life line God used people in authority in Ifaki Grammar School to provide while I passed through the institution. To God be all the glory for later doing greater things than all the above in my life.

Tajudeen K. Jinadu wrote:
….Chief Adeoya was so versatile. He was a master of virtually every subject taught in our school in those days, from English Language (including) phonetics, Latin, History, Mathematics, Music etc and these he would teach in any class in the school. He would readily fill in the gap for any absentee teacher even without prior notice! I was privileged apart from being his student and time keeper in my time, I was also a teacher under his watch. Those who knew him or who passed through this great man who gave his all for our school cannot but continue to appreciate him. On hindsight I will rate him the best. I am sure that some of us who were a little naughty in those days cannot forget his canes which were meant to always keep us in tow. How about his behaviour to the security men who were always sleeping on duty!

Some of the teachers were sponsored to the university by either the school or the Methodist mission. The school got them fresh, and we took the best out them. Many of them were really great and very devoted. They coached us privately as the WASCE exams were approaching. I can remember Mr Fabelurin as we gathered in his backyard while teaching us history without any notebook, Mr Oni (soliloquy) teaching English and literature while baba Adetunmbi (the senior tutor) taught us Geography and the Yoruba language. I must say my only distinction was in Yoruba.

Dr. Folorunso Ajayi wrote:
In 1968 when I started in form one, IGS had become an established school which parents wanted their children to attend. They were usually fascinated by the beauty of the school's electricity conferred by a generator which lit up the campus at night. During the day, the school uniform of checked green shirts over beige khaki shorts made the students beautiful.

The school compound was clean and trees lined its network of roads. The ambience was serene, interrupted only by the excited cries of playful students and the thrice a day beating of the drum that announced to students that meals were ready. One of the first things a new student noticed was the fancy nicknames of most senior boys. There was *Emperor* - Okoma in the football team, Senior *Windy* - Badamosi, the fastest sprinter, *Padua* - the jovial Senior Adeosun, *Alanga Tugara* - Adeogun, *Atuma* - the sportsman, Akinsanya and Senior *Ewuare* named after an Oba of the ancient Benin Kingdom. The more fanciful names however ended with the vowel '*o*' such as *Opisco Buffalo* - footballer, *Omosco Filando* - Dele Filani, and our amiable Biology teacher, Mr. Bankole whose nickname was '*Banko*.

Each weekday started with pupils in forms 1-3 drawing water to the dining hall for cooking and washing purposes. Occasionally in exceptionally dry harmattan seasons, we supplemented this by going directly across the Ifaki-Iworoko road to fetch water from a brook that always seemed never to run dry. Each student in forms 1 and 2 was assigned to a "senior" – a form five student. After that, we gathered in our dormitories for an early morning devotion of hymn singing and prayers, conducted by a senior boy. Next came breakfast. Students were summoned by the beating of a drum. Five flat notes of *doom-doom-doom, doom doom* announced that the table was ready. Occasionally four notes with two quick finishes (*doom-doom-do-doom*) indicated that water was required for cooking and forms 1 and 2 students who had not taken their obligatory two buckets to the dining hall would scamper to perform their duty, otherwise they might be barred from eating.

The four House captains sat with their juniors but the other four school prefects shared a single, separate table with the Senior Prefect – the *High Table* at the top end of the dining hall. Any ill or absent student would have his meal shared out as "*extras*" but a pupil who knew that a friend was absent from school would go and collect the absentee's plate before others got wind of such booties. Sunday night was the best day as we had bread and stew with a tiny cut of beef in the morning, boiled yams for lunch and boiled rice and beans with a boiled egg each for supper. An egg with a meal was a delicacy in those days.

The daily routine roughly includes 7:30 – Breakfast; 8 am – Morning assembly. 8:10 – Classes began. Each lesson lasted 40 minutes; 10:10-10:30 – Toilet Break. 12:30-12:40 – *Recess (a ten-minute break)*. 2pm (14:00h) – School over. Lunch 3-4pm – Afternoon Siesta. 4:30-5:30pm – Preparation (*prep*). 6pm – Supper. 7:30-9pm – Evening Preparation. 9pm – Night assembly (conducted by the seniors and prefects). 10pm – "Lights Out." The generator was switched off after a prior warning 5 minutes earlier. This arrangement ensured that each student got 8 hours of sleep at night, an hour's rest after lunch, time for physical exercise, for institutionised instruction and personal study. On Fridays: Forms 1-3 would remain in the assembly hall to learn one new hymn. Saturdays: After breakfast, the prefects supervised forms 1-4 in environmental sanitation – cleaning the school compound, cutting the grass and washing the toilets and bathrooms. Sundays: Students dressed up in their Sunday attire: a white '*buba*' on a white long pant, '*sokoto.*' We filed in groups to town to attend churches of our denomination – Anglican, Methodist or Catholic. The fear of Mr. Tsephe ensured nobody lingered in town or wander off to MGHS – our sister, all-girls' school at the opposite end of town.

Athletics and football were the dominant sports. Mr. Bankole brought out long-stored hockey sticks and got students interested. We entered a regional competition but were knocked out narrowly in the first round by Victory College, Ikare, they won 2-1 on our own pitch. The school year in Nigeria's secondary schools ran from January to December up till 1972. It was in 1973 that the format changed from January to December to today's September to June to synchronise with university semesters.

Athletics practice normally started as soon as students resumed in January. Tracks would be marked out by sand fetched by junior students. The inter-house sports competition took place in the second term (April/May) and Jones House was the perennial winner. However, in 1967 and the following four years, School House hit a purple patch as they upstaged Jones House through the sheer efforts of an amazing prodigy from Ikole in the person of Ebenezer Oludare Akinsanya.

The Western Region in those days had an annual football competition called the Principals' Cup. Contiguous schools would be grouped together to compete in mini leagues until zonal winners met at the divisional finals at Ado-Ekiti to crown a winner (usually Christ's School) would play the champion from Akoko (usually Victory College). The Ondo provincial champions would go on to Ibadan where the provincial champions played a knockout competition over about ten days in June. The best players would be selected to form the Western Academicals to face Bendel, East and Northern regional champions. From these, a Nigerian team would be selected to face Ghana Academicals. It was in pursuit of this dream that Akinsanya single-handedly dragged IGS past Aiyede Grammar School in 1971. We needed a win to advance but were drawing nil-nil until two minutes left to play. Akinsanya, nursing a sore right foot received from running spikes in athletics, maneuvered the ball to his good foot and curled a beauty into the corner of the net. We went wild in delirious celebrations.

170

The school was governed by the principal, house masters, prefects and the senior boys in form 5. The principal, *Olotu*, was resident on the campus. His house at the eastern end of the school was situated somewhat between the dining hall and School House. House masters lived in two semi-detached houses beside Alarada and IPU dormitories. Prefects were elected in November each year just as final year students were commencing their final examinations, the West African School Certificate Examinations (WASCE). It became WAEC in 1973 (West African Examinations Council). To ensure that a prefect would not be handicapped by the encumbrances of office, prefects were chosen from amongst those students who had placed in positions 1st to 10th in each stream in the second term examinations in year 4. On election day, all pupils would be invited to write the names of nine boys who they wanted as prefects. Usually, the boy with the most nominations was elected the Senior Prefect, *SP*. There would be four House Captains and four School Prefects for Food, Sports, Labour and the Chapel.

By 1968, the school was instructing students in the following subjects: Arts and Humanities – History, Geography, History, Bible Knowledge, Mathematics, Additional Mathematics Languages – Yoruba, English Language, English Literature. Sciences – **Biology**, Chemistry and Physics. French was taught only to forms 1-3 students. Agricultural Science was taught to forms 1-4 but not offered at the WASCE. All students in years 1-3 were instructed in all the disciplines but at the beginning of year 4, each student was allowed to choose 8 or 9 subjects for their final examinations as long as they included the compulsory subjects of English Language, Mathematics and Biology.

In the early years of the school, science subjects were not offered but the likes of senior Adekunle Ajaja, Mr Biodun Agbelese and others went on to study these subjects in university through devoted personal tutelage and they excelled as physicists, chemists and assorted scientists. Mr Ajaja in particular was the school's academic prodigy and yardstick. He was so clever that in his first year at school, he gained a double promotion (as we called it), being catapulted to start in form three the following year. By the time he reached form 5, the school duration had been shortened to five years so he wrote his WASCE after only four years of study. In spite of this, he achieved a Grade One with an aggregate score of 13 in his finals which remained the school record, until 1972 when it was lowered to 11. I was glad when I heard that it didn't take another ten years for another student to beat my own record. In my final year at Ifaki, I certainly had the belief that the products of our school could match their counterparts at Christ's School, the Ibadan or Lagos schools and their equivalents in ability, if not in experience.

171

With that belief, I wrote the 1973 concessional entry examinations for the preliminary courses of the University of Ibadan. Among the 25,000 Nigerian students who sat for that examination, I came 4th as revealed by the Admissions Officer of the university. I had gone from Ifaki to Government College, Ibadan for Higher School Certificate but abandoned that in favour of a concessional entry to the UI. At Government College, I was thrust into a class that included four boys who had each scored 6 aggregates – the pinnacle of academic excellence at that level – in the same WASCE in which I had 11 at Ifaki. The first two were my classmates at Ibadan university's Faculty of Medicine. IGS has produced and will yet produce graduates who can rub shoulders with any student in Nigeria.

Olotu (Chief J O Adeoya the principal) gathers the school choir together. He puts them through their paces as they learn to sing The Halleluiah Chorus a piece from Handell's Messiah. The harmattan is coming and the grass is browning from lack of rain. The final year students are uninvolved as they were busy with their WASCE. As the choir gets to grips with mastering their piece, noises are coming from the football pitch as IPU house tangles with School House in the inter-house football competition. The prize for the winner is the right to face the perennial winners, Jones House, who dispatched Alarada the night before. Elsewhere, anxious students are revising for the promotion exams. All these do not stop the "Strong Boys" in form three from going to town without exeat. They will try their luck at Oke Odo where fishes are to be caught. Baba Omotunde is strict but some girls want adventure. Baba Tsephe, in his Peugeot 403 must not catch these stowaways.....

Back to the Assembly Hall and the choir. The pianists - three of them support the principal. Baba Adetunmbi, Chief G O Dada "Mekaiko" and Mr Ajibola are all accomplished keyboard players. The D Day arrives. IGS boys march to Methodist Church, Ilogbe. The Oke-Odo girls from the MGHS are already seated. Boys on one side, girls on the other. The congregation, Ifaki senior citizens separate the lecherous duo. The choir is eager and the service commences with the priest on duty praying. This service is called The Festival of Readings and Carols, an annual fest. The Halleluiah chorus rings out. It is divine. Then a Bible passage is read out. More carols -Sing Lullaby, I saw a maiden, Rom-Pompom, I saw three ships come sailing by, etc …Then, I was called to read the fifth lesson, Isaiah 11:1-9. I put a strong emphasis on the last phrase, "As the waters cover the sea." And my seniors acclaim me. The passage is traditionally reserved for a Form One student and Olotu chose me that year.

We went for Christmas break. I went searching for the lyrics of the Hallelujah chorus. I was not a member of the choir. But I like the singing. And still do. Over five decades later, I've mastered the chorus, read that Isaiah passage over and over again. Thanks to Olotu, I got hooked on Methodist hymns. I am an Anglican and a Pentecostal but in my library, I have the Methodist Hymn Book, its 1990 revised edition and its music edition. I now like to read the history behind Christian popular hymns and of their authors. Which brings me to a carol that I only knew in 2019, and is now one of my top 3 Christmas Carols (alongside Good King Wenceslas because of their deep and didactic scriptural messages.

O HOLY NIGHT: In 1843, the French wine merchant and poet, Placide Cappeau, was asked to write a Christmas poem to celebrate the recent renovation of the organ in the church of his home town of Roquemaure, Gard. He wasn't particularly religious but he obliged, writing the poem whose opening line was: Minuit, chrétiens! c'est l'heure, solennelle"(Midnight, Christians, is the solemn hour)." Cappeau would have followed his father into vinification - wine making - but for a gun accident which resulted in amputation of his right hand. He turned to writing). He had socialist views. Note the lines "…to set slaves free… they are our brothers…" which, advocating for the manumission of slaves in 19th-century France, would have been frowned upon by bourgeois slave owners.

In 1847, Adolphe Adam, a French composer and music critic, set the poem to music. The resulting work, 'O Holy Night" is now a popular Christmas carol. But the amazing thing was that a man who was said to be non-religious would capture the essence of the Christmas message so accurately, acknowledging that Jesus Christ is the son of God, sent to the world to save sinners by removing "the original stain" and he is the Coming King that we must bow to, and worship! Minuit, chrétiens c'est l'heure solennelle; Où l'Homme Dieu descendu jusqu'à nous Pour effacer la tache originelle…(Midnight, Christians, is the solemn hour; Where the Man God came down to us, To erase the original stain…) Nearly a decade later, in 1855, the lyrics were translated into English by Minister John Sullivan Dwight into what we sing today.

Away from the melody, let us think of the salient truth behind Placide Cappeau's poem that reminds and reassures us that God sent His son into our world to cleanse our original stain. Christmas is good, but don't forget what it is and why we celebrate it: God sent his only begotten son into our world to save us from our sins and from God's punishment for unrepented sin. Are YOU washed in the blood of the Lamb? You've got your Covid vaccine; have you got the "Sin vaccine" by being born again (John3:3) by believing in Jesus, whose birth Christmas celebrates? Please do TODAY.

173

"Find out who you are and be that person.
That's what your soul was put on this earth to be.
Find that truth, live that truth, and everything else
will come."
Ellen Degeneres

EPILOGUE

What I have tried to do in this book is to book is primarily to have a one-stop book on the history of secondary school education in Nigeria. Essentially to tell the stories of the schools that produced the best of Nigerian brains and distinguished personalities who have excelled within and outside Nigeria. More importantly to remind us that we have got it right in the past and yet the feat can be relived and sustained if only the present crop of leaders in government could let the right calibre of people take charge of our affairs.

One thing is certain, the positive impact of access to good quality education can never be overemphasised. Those who had access to Western education for instance had significant inter-generational impacts. Majority of the individuals who were part of the beneficiaries of education at the colonial schools had higher living standards and better social networks compared to uneducated individuals. The educated individuals were also much less likely to become peasants and much more likely to be politically active. The sad commentary is the drifting Nigerian system which has relegated educated ones to the background and turned the hard-working ones to appear "lazy" (*so alagbara di ole*) because they can't make ends meet due to the collapsed system and truncated egalitarian society.

Relatively, there were disparities in access to education based on region, gender, and religion. Localities that had higher levels of public investment in the early colonial years continued to have higher levels of investment in later periods, leading to huge economic activities up till today in some areas. The most disturbing trend is the system that continues to kill merit for mediocracy. Strategic government positions are given disproportionately, and skewed towards less competent ones with sound education and good proficient exposure.

Disparities have also tended to persist into post-colonial times creating intelligentsia and political elite. While a sect saw education as a source of empowerment and demanded more of it, some part hinges their progress on the undue political influence with their ability to get whatever they want irrespective of their qualification for as long as their kinsmen are in government and in "power". The relegation of merit is dampening the spirit of the people so avid for education, where without being a prig, children are more anxious to go to school. My charge to all is that, in education there lays your honour, no one should be discouraged. Emergence of indigenous political elite is one of the benefits of exposure to good quality education in the colonial days. Some of the early educated Nigerians went on to lead anti-colonial movements, the pan-African movement, and linked their struggles to the international socialist movement. Besides, good education prepares one to be an international citizen such that one will be in position to excel in well organised system that provides equal opportunities for all irrespective of race and creed.

In Nigeria, resentment in some quarters and the need to complement the missionary/private schools ultimately led to the institution of the Free Primary Education scheme in the 1950s among other political considerations. It was the biggest expansion of education in colonial Africa, nearly doubling the number of primary schools in the region between 1952 and 1954. Over 50 percent of children between the ages of six and twelve years were beneficiaries of the free education of the old Western Region according published government reports. It provided a wider base for entrants into secondary schools, trade schools and teacher training colleges, which quickened the pace of the development of middle-level manpower. In contrast to 1954 when one out of five pupils in primary school was a girl, by 1966, almost two out of five were girls. In all, the free primary education created positive spillovers for the labor market and the economy. In places where education was available, it became a source of empowerment for Africans.

The task before the Nigerian government today is the fall in the standard of education at all levels, especially in all government schools. A Standard Six certificate holder in the colonial days was far more educated than a school certificate holder of the 21st century in Nigeria. The university lecturers were still on strike for over 3 months as at the time of publishing this book. It is the sustainable excellence associated with schools and not age of schools that matters. It is hoped that this book will touch the heart of the enemies of progress in Nigeria to give deprivation of the masses a break.

Some of us, our parents wanted us or actually made sure that we attended the schools that they had the privilege of attending for mentoring. Today, many of the people in this category are grateful to their parents for the rare privilege of being part of a worthy heritage. The reality today is that not many of us can send our children to the good primary and secondary schools we attended in as much as some of us would have wished to do. It is not only sad but it reminds us of the extent which things have gone bad in Nigeria of today and how the successive governments have failed us. It is a complete let-down.

The old students of a number of schools have intervened e.g. CMS Grammar School, KC Lagos, Igbobi College to mention a few. Intervention is in progress in some other schools. The Anglican schools in Lagos are back to the mission and the standard of the schools are gradually being upgraded under the respective administrations of all the schools and the proprietors. Ekiti government too returned some schools to their original owners. The truth is that the task is enormous for the majority of these schools and it is beyond the capacity of the alumni and the original owners to turn the situation around for better. Most of the stolen public money kept away in overseas banks and the ill-gotten wealth by the thieving Nigerian elites are more than enough to take care of the needs in the public schools in Nigeria. Nigeria as a country is certainly unhinged! Until the nation is healed of the festering ailment there may be no end to the depleting state of public utilities and infrastructures in our schools generally, the universities inclusive.

The long and short of it is that, the expansion of quality education remains an urgent necessity, to enable Nigeria realise her full potentials as a nation so endowed with a huge human resource base.

"If you want to know how much you'll be missed when you are gone, put your finger in a bucket of water and then remove it. The hole that's left will be how much you are missed." No one is irreplaceable. No one. You may not leave a hole, but you can leave a mark on a person, a team, or a culture that lives on after you're gone. You may not be missed but you can be remembered--in the best possible way."

© **Mansueto** Ventures LLC. (*Written on 30;12/2013*)

ANNEX

A Directory of Old Generation Secondary Schools in Nigeria 1885-1973

S/N	Name of School	Founded	The Founder
1	Baptist Academy	1885	Baptist Mission
2	CMS Grammar School, Bariga, Lagos	1859	Anglican (CMS)
3	Methodist Boys High School, Lagos	1878	Methodist Mission
4	Methodist Girls High School, Yaba, Lagos	1879	Methodist Mission
5	Hope Waddell Training Institute, Calabar	1896	United Presbyterian
6	St. Anne's School, Ibadan	1895	Anglican
7	Oron Boy's High School, Oron	1897	Anglican
8	St. Paul's College, Iyenu, Awka	1900	Anglican
9	Etinam Institute Etinan, Akwa Ibom	1902	
10	Wesley College of Science, Ibadan	1905	Methodist
11	Methodist Boy's High School, Oron	1905	Methodist
12	Abeokuta Grammar School, Idi-Aba	1908	Anglican
13	King's College, Lagos	1909	Federal Government
14	St. John's School, Bida	1909	Anglican
15	Alhuda-Huda College, Zaria	1910	Government
16	Ijebu-Ode Grammar School	1913	Anglican
17	Eko Boys High School, Mushin, Lagos	1913	Methodist
18	Ibadan Grammar School, Molete, Ibadan	1913	Anglican
19	Government Secondary School, Ilorin	1914	Government
20	Government College, Katsina-Ala, Benue	1915	Government
21	Etinan Institute, Etinan, Akwa-Ibom	1915	Qua Iboe Mission
22	Ondo Boys High School, Ondo	1919	Anglican
23	Duke Town Secondary School	1919	Qua Iboe Mission
24	Government College, Kaduna	1920	Government

24	Murtala Muhammed College, Yola	1920	
26	Baptist Boys High School, Abeokuta	1923	Baptist Mission
27	Methodist College, Uzuakoli, Abia	1923	Methodist Mission
28	Ibo Boys' High School, Uzuakoli, Abia	1923	Anglican Mission
29	Dennis Memorial Grammar School, Onitsha	1925	Anglican Mission
30	Queens College, Yaba, Lagos	1927	Government
31	Government College, Ibadan	1927	Government
32	Government College, Umuahia, Abia	1927	Government
33	Barewa College, Zaria	1921	Government
34	United Memorial Grammar School, Ibadan	1928	Christian Mission
35	St. Gregory College, Ikoyi, Lagos	1928	Catholic Mission
36	St. Thomas College, Ibusa	1928	Anglican Mission
37	St. Charles College, Onitsha	1929	Anglican Mission
38	Aggrey Memorial College, Arochukwu	1931	Alvan Ikoku
39	Igbobi College, Yaba, Lagos	1931	Anglican & Methodist
40	St' Theresa College, Oke-Ado, Ibadan	1932	Catholic Mission
41	Oduduwa Grammar School, Ile-Ife	1932	Anglican Mission
42	Christ the King College, Onitsha, Anambra	1933	Catholic Mission
43	Christ's School, Ado-Ekiti	1933	Anglican Mission
44	Ilesha Grammar School, Ilesha	1934	Community
45	St. Patrick's College, Calabar	1934	Catholic Mission
46	Holy Rosary College, Enugu	1935	Catholic Mission
47	Dennius Memorial, Onitsha	1935	
48	Government Secondary School, Owerri	1935	Government
49	Edo College, Benin City	1937	Government
50	Ibadan Boys High School, Ibadan	1938	Chief T.L. Oyesina
51	Baptist High School, Bodija, Ibadan	1940	Baptist Mission
52	Reagan Memorial Baptist Girls Sch, Lagos	1941	
53	Queen of the Rosary College, Onitsha	1942	Catholic Mission
54	African Church School, Kajola, Ifo	1943	Christian Mission

55	Lisabi Grammar School, Abeokuta	1943	Community
56	Offa Grammar School, Offa	1943	Community
57	Olivet Baptist High, Oyo	1945	Baptist Mission
58	Adeola Odutola College	1945	Chief Odutola
59	Government College, Ughelli	1945	Government
60	Anglican Girls' Grammar School, Lagos	1945	Anglican Mission
61	Urhobo College, Effurun	1946	Community
62	Remo Secondary School, Sagamu	1946	
63	Ansar–Ud–Deen Comprehensive College, Otta	1946	Islamic Mission
64	Imade College, Owo	1946	Community
65	Victory College, Ikare, Ondo	1947	
66	Hussey College, Warri	1947	
67	Emmanuel College, Owerri		Christian Mission
68	Ahmaddiya (Anwar-ul-Islam) College, Lagos	1948	Islamic Mission
69	Stella Mary's College, Port Harcourt	1948	
70	Government College, Keffi	1949	Government
71	Molusi College, Ijebu-Igbo	1949	
72	Baptist High School, Borokiri, Port Harcourt	1949	Baptist Mission
73	Oriwu College, Ikorodu	1949	
74	Ago-Iwoye Secondary School, Ago-Iwoye	1950	
75	Ijebu Muslim College	1950	Islamic Mission
76	St. Peter Claver's College, Sapele	1950	Christian Mission
77	Egbado (Yewa) College, Ilaro	1950	
77	St. Thomas's Aquinas College, Akure	1951	Catholic Mission
78	Titcombe College, Egbe	1951	Christian Mission
79	Queen's School, Ibadan	1952	Government
80	Government College, Afikpo, Ebonyi	1952	Government
81	Oyemekun Grammar School, Akure	1953	Anglican Mission
82	St. Margaret Girls School Ilesha	1953	Christian Mission
83	Sapele Boys Academy	1953	Okotie-Eboh

181

84	Lagos City College,	1953	Dr Nnamdi Azikiwe
85	St. Anthony's Grammar School, Ijebu-Imushin	1954	Christian Mission
86	Loyola College, Ibadan	1954	Catholic Mission
87	St. Bernadine's, Oyo	1954	
89	Our Lady of Apostles Second. Sch. Ijebu-Ode	1954	Catholic Mission
90	Manuwa Memorial Grammar School, Iju-Odo	1954	
91	Fiditi Grammar School, Fiditi, Oyo	1954	
92	National High School, Arondizuogu, Imo	1954	
93	Iheme Memorial Grammar Sch, Arondizuogu	1954	
94	St. Louis Secondary School, Ondo	1954	Christian Mission
95	Gboluji Grammar School, Ile-Oluji, Ondo	1954	
66	Ekiti Parapo College, Ido-Ekiti	1954	Ekiti Community
97	Badagry Grammar School, Badagry	1955	
98	Doherty Memorial Grammar Sch, Ijero- Ekiti	1955	
99	African Church Grammar School, Abeokuta	1955	Christian Mission
100	Ibara Anglican High School, Abeokuta	1955	Anglican Mission
101	St Patrick's College, Asaba	1955	Christian Mission
102	St. Monica Girls' School, Ondo	1955	Christian Mission
103	Gbongan/Odeomu Ang. Gram. Scl, Gbongan	1955	Anglican Mission
104	Our Lady of Apostles Secondary School, Lagos	1956	Catholic Mission
105	St. Catherine's Anglican Girls School, Owo	1956	Anglican Mission
106	St Joseph's College, Ondo	1956	Christian Mission
107	Methodist High School, Okitipupa	1956	Methodist Church
108	Mayflower School, Ikenne	1956	Dr Tai Solarin
109	Isoyin Grammar School, Isoyin	1956	
110	St. Joseph College, Ondo	1956	Christian Mission
111	Yejide Girls Grammar School, Ibadan	1956	
112	Methodist High School, Ilesa	1956	Methodist Mission
113	Ekiti Baptist High School	1956	
114	Ebenezer Grammar School, Abeokuta	1957	

115	Odogbolu Grammar School, Odogbolu	1957	
116	Ifaki Grammar School, Ifaki-Ekiti	1957	Community
117	Notre Dame College, Ozoro	1957	Catholic Mission
118	Government College, Makurdi	1957	Government
119	Holy Rosary College, Idah	1957	Christian Mission
120	Anglican Grammar School, Iju-Itaogbolu	1957	Anglican Mission
121	African Church Grammar School, Oka-Akoko	1957	Christian Mission
122	Aiyede Grammar School, Aiyede-Ekiti	1957	Community
123	Annunciation Grammar School, Ikere-Ekiti	1957	Catholic Mission
124	Olofin Anglican Grammar School, Idanre	1957	Anglican Mission
125	Igbo Elerin Grammar School, Ibadan	1957	
126	Okemesi Grammar School, Okemesi-Ekiti	1958	Community
127	Lagelu Grammar School, Ibadan	1958	
128	Ahmadu Bahago Secondary School, Niger	1958	Baptist Mission
129	Anglican Grammar School, Igbara-Oke	1958	Anglican Mission
130	Ise-Emure Grammar School	1958	
131	Ayedaade Grammar School, Ikire	1958	
132	Akinorun Grammar School, Ikirun	1958	
133	St. Patrick's College, Oka-Akoko	1959	Christian Mission
134	Ondo Anglican Grammar School, Ondo	1959	Anglican Mission
135	Origbo Community High School, Ipetumodu	1959	
136	Premier Grammar School, Abeokuta	1959	
137	Ansar Ud Deen High School, Ikole	1959	Islamic Mission
138	Fiwasaiye Girls Grammar School, Akure	1960	Anglican Mission
139	Adventist Grammar School, Ede	1960	Anglican Mission
140	Ado Grammar School, Ado-Ekiti	1960	
141	Edo Boys' High School, Benin	1960	
142	St Charles Catholic Grammar Sch, Oshogbo	1961	Christian Mission
143	Amoye Grammar School, Ikere-Ekiti	1961	
144	Methodist Girls High School, Ifaki-Ekiti	1961	Methodist Church

145	St Louis, Ikere-Ekiti	1961	Christian Mission
146	Covenant Comprehensive Sch Port Harcourt	1962	Christian Mission
147	International School, Ibadan	1963	Private School
148	Comprehensive High School, Aiyetoro	1963	Govt/Foreign Aid
149	Moba Grammar School, Otun	1965	
150	Government College Bida		
151	Anglican Grammar School		
152	Notre Dame, Usi-Ekiti		Catholic Mission
153	Egbado College, Ilaro		
154	Egbado Methodist High School, Igbogila		Methodist Church
155	Nazareth High School, Imeko		Christian Mission
156	Government College Bida		Government
157	Methodist Comprehensive High Sch Aaye	1973	Methodist Church

APPENDIX – Graphical Illustrations

i. **Primary School Enrollment (1950)**

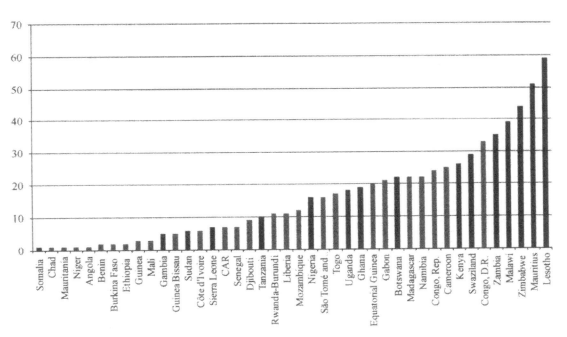

Figure I. *Gross primary-school enrolment rates (age 5–14) subdivided by British (black) and non-British (grey) African colonies, 1950.*
Source: UNESCO, Statistical Yearbook 1964, table 9.

ii.   **British Colonies: Missionary Schools**

Nigeria, Southern	59,002	200,342	91.1	97
Mauritius	9,635	24,607	50.6	61.6
Uganda	11,954[a]	267,837	100	98.9
Nyasaland	61,091[a]	206,202	100	99.9
Kenya	2,432	129,101	100	92.2
Tanganyika		66,753		85.6
N. Rhodesia	2,400[a]	122,312	100	99.2
S. Rhodesia		ns		ns
Bechuanaland	2,236	14,239	100	98.4
Total/weighted average	170,638	1,179,993	93.3	95.5

Source: Online Supplementary material, table A1.

Notes: [a]Sierra Leone 1890, Southern Nigeria 1914, Uganda 1905, Nyasaland 1905. The figure for Northern and Southern Rhodesia in 1900 is a guesstimate for the combined territories of Rhodesia.

iii.   **Disparities: Unequal Investments in Education**

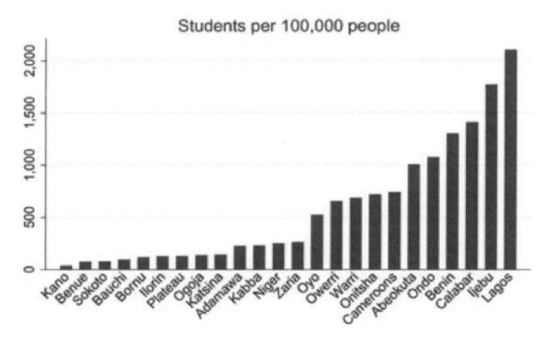

iv.   Gender Disparities

Table Average attendance in Government primary schools in 1928.

Province	N of Sch.	Boys	Girls	Total	% of Girls
Colony	5	584	79	663	11.9%
Benin	14	1,994	136	2,130	6.3%
Calabar	6	1,356	67	1,423	4.7%
Ijebu	---	---	---	---	---
Ogoja	2	225	17	272	6.2%
Ondo	1	132	13	145	8.9%
Onitsha	3	781	24	805	2.9%
Owerri	7	1,512	107	1,619	6.6%
Oyo	1	197	28	225	12.4%
Warri	4	707	105	812	12.9%
Total	49	8,440	703	9,143	7.6%

iii.   Curriculum: Nigeria

Syllabus for primary schools 1909 (Code of Education, 1909)

Obligatory subjects for boys	Obligatory subjects for girls
Colloquial English and Nature study	None
Reading with translation into vernacular, meaning of words and simple Grammar	Same as boys
Arithmetic	Same as boys
Hygiene and sanitation	Same as boys
Manual Training to include drawing or shorthand from standard III	Domestic Economy – Cookery or Bakery, Plain Needlework and Laundry.
Moral Instruction	Same as boys
Optional subjects	**Optional subjects**
History and Geography	None
Singing	Same as boys
Drill and physical exercise	Same as boys

Source: Okonkwo & Ezeh, 2008

"It had long since come to my attention that people of accomplishment rarely sat back and let things happen to them.
They went out and happened to things."
Learnado Da Vinci

ACKNOLEDGEMENTS

This is a product of many years of research on the materials I have been keeping as I came across them online and through interactions with a wide range of people. Therefore, my acknowledgement goes to all the articles and other materials searched on the internet. Also, to the various individuals that I interacted with, over the years on one-on-one or through on-line interactive forums, from which some facts were got which were used in this book.

The last two weeks to finalizing this book was kind of terrific with intensive fact finding and writings because I wanted to get the book ready before my 60th birthday on July 2022. I must appreciate every alumnus of schools that I contacted to get information on their alma mater. Thanks for tolerating my last-minute clarifications through calls and WhatsApp. The fact that you responded to my inquiries further encouraged to see the project through and that the book is worth the effort. We did together, I thank each and every one of you, too numerous to mention because I don't want to risk any omission.

I participated in the virtual course of Wheeler Institute for Business and Development at London Business School on African History through the Lens of Economics between 1st of February and 12th of April in 2022. I found some of the lecture materials useful while writing this book. In particular I must acknowledge the papers of Léonard Wantchékon on Education and Human Capital in Colonial Africa Scramble for Africa - Country Focus: Nigeria and the scholarly presentation of Nonso Obikili. Also, the research work of C. O. Taiwo is hereby acknowledged.

I must appreciate my beloved and very supportive wife, Mrs Olabowale Adetunmbi for her assistance while putting finishing touches to this book. She is a product of one of the heritage secondary schools written about in this book. A conducive home front has made it easy for me to add this book to the stable of my literary works. I love you loads.

What is it the at we have which is not given to us by God almighty? I give God the glory for the great things He has done, most importantly for the rare grace of the capacity to write yet another book and the uncommon enablement He granted me to make it happen. Thank you Lord. I also appreciate the feedbacks I get from those who have read my books.

Seye Adetunmbi, 18/7/22

INDEX

A

Abati, Reuben 76
Abdulrazaq 39,40
Abeokuta Grammar School, 30
Abiodun, Dapo 71
Abiola, Kola 102
Abridged Biographies 7
Achebe, Chinua 46
Acknowledgements 189
Adadevoh, Stella 86
Adamolekun, Ladipo 69,
Adebayo - Adeniyi 22, Adeyinka 35,67
    Sola 49
Adebo, Simeon 32
Adeboye, Enock 73
Adebutu 20
Adedeji, Dokun 70
Adefarasin, Paul 50
Adefope 22
Adegboye, Ogoga 67
Ade-John, Oyin 67
Adelegan 23
Adeleye, Kunle 71
Adelodun 27
Ademola, Adetokunbo 32
Adelabu - Adegoke 44, Modupe 70
Ademola, Adetokunbo 47
Adenuga 36,102
Adeloye, Adelola 68,142
Adeola, Fola 27
Adeolu, Funso 26
Aderinnokun 48
Adesanya, Abraham 34
Adesina, Lam 91
Adesokan, Elkanah 68

Adesola, Bola 80
Adesoye College, Offa 115
Adetunmbi – Dayo 71, David 13, 37, 67,
  88, 118-122 Labo 75, Olubunmi 89,131,
    Seye 2, 189
Adeyemi, Lamidi Alaafin 48
Adigun 44
Adu, Jab 48
Aduwo 50
Afonja, Similolu 69
Agagu 36
Aganga, Segun 66,70,159
Agbakoba 52
Agbaje – Jimi 48, Segun 47
Agbetuyi 9
AIONIAN 72
Ajayi - Ade J.F. 49,67 Adesuyi 71
     Eniola 71, Funso 131,168-173
     Kemi 71,94 Yomi 79 Wura 71
Ajekigbe, Moyo 70
Ajomale 10
Aka-Bashorun 35
Ake 33
Akeju 7,70
Akeredolu Rotimi 91
Akinbanji, Mofe 71
Akindele, Bode 76
Akingbola, Erastus 70
Akinola – Dotun 91 Jonathan 67
Akintoye 68
Akinyede 48
Akinyemi, Bolaji 50
Akisanya, Titi 80
Akomolafe, Ade 88

Akpata 33
Alabi, Kayode 78
Alade, Fola, 68
Alakija, Adeyemo 47
Alele-Williams 42
Allagoa 52
Aluko – Samuel 67, Bolaji 70,145,157
American International School, Abuja 115
Amosun 10
Aniagolu 52
Anikulapo-Kuti, Fela 30, Femi 20
Apostle of Harmony 10
Applied Knowledge 8
Araka, Emmanuel 73
Asabia, Samuel 67
Asebiomo -Alfred 55,67,88 Bose 88,89
Awogbade, Soji 70
Awolowo, H.I.D. 27, Segun 44,49,50
Awosika 27
Azikiwe 16,26
B
Babalakin 44
Babamboni 55
Babatola – Adenike 71, Joel 67
Babington-Ashaye 76
Bakare, Tunde 76
Bamgboye, Dola 23
Bamidele, Opeyemi 20
Bank-Anthony, Mobolaji 20, 34
Balewa
Baptist Academy 14, 19
Barewa College 39
Belgore – Alfa 73 Dele
Bello, Ahmadu 40

Bello, Dele 78
Bello-Osagie 32,33
Balogun, Subomi 49,50
Borokini, Simeon 76
British colonial admin 14 41
British colony and missionary schools 186
British International School, Lagos 115
C
Chopde 99
Christianity and Anglicanism 8
Christ's School, Ado-Ekiti 13,14,53-71, 138
Christ's School and others 147
Christ's School and sports 155
Christ the King College 51
Ciroma 40
Comprehensive High School, Aiyetoro 101
Corona Secondary School, Lagos 115
CMS 21
CMS Grammar School 14,21,24
Crowther 21
D
Dallimore 53
Dasuki 39,40
Day Waterman College 115
Dikko 39
Directory of old generation secondary schools in Nigeria 179
Dowen College, Lekki, Lagos 115
E
Edo College, Benin 74
Ekitipanupo 10
Ekiti Parapo College 15,88

Eko Boys High School 35
Ekwueme - Alex 32,33 Hellen 81
    Lazarus 46
Elegushi 27
Elias – Gbolahan 50, Teslim 49
El-Rufai 40
Ekwensi, Cyprian 44
Emmanuel, Francesca 80
Emiabata – Niyi 50 Yewande 80
Emiola, Tinu 66
Enahoro 32
Enwonwu 46
Epilogue 175
Erediauwa 44
Eso – Kayode 72 Ladipo 7,72
Etinan Institute 37
Ewuare, Oba of Benin 74
F
Fafowora, Akin 73
Fagbenro-Byron 44
Fajemirokun 10,91
Falegan, Samuel 143
Famosaya 66,84,137,161
Fanadez, Dehinde 48
Farounbi, Yemi 71
Fashola 35,50
Fasuan 68
Fayemi - Bisi 27, Kayode 71 Segun 50
Fayose 79
Federal Government Colleges in Nigeria
111-115
Financial Intermediation and Practice 9
Fiwasaye Anglican Girls School 97
French colonial admin 14

G
Gbadamosi 26
Gbajabiamila 50
George – Ayo 48 Bode 34
Government College Ibadan 43
Government College Umahia 45
Government schools 14
Gowon 40
Grange High School 115
Greenoak International College, Port
Harcourt 115
Greenspring School Lagos 115
H
Heritage private secondary schools in
Nigeria 115
Hillcrest School, Jos 115
Holy Child College, Lagos 80
Hope Waddel 28
I
Ibiam 28
Ibori, James 74
Ibrahim, Ado 37
Ibru – Alex 36, Felix 50, Michael 49
Ifaki Grammar School 13,14,118-135,
164-173
Igbobi College 49
Igbinedion – Gabriel 35 Lucky 74
Ige 36
Ighodalo 32,33
Ijebu-ode Grammar School
Ilesa Grammar School 72
Ilube 74
Iluyomade 37
International Community School, Abuja
115

International School Ibadan 103
Irokefe 47
Ita, Anya Eyo 28
Itsueli, Justus Uduimo 55,69
Iyayi, Macauley 62,69
J
Jakande 31
Jegede – Tayo 85 Wale 87
Jinadu – Kunle 55, Taju 167 Yewande 80
Johnson, Mobolaji 26
K
Kalu, Orji 46
Kelani 30
King's College 31
Kolade 44,68
Kudeti 24
Kumuyi 94
L
Lagos Anglican Girls Grammar School 92
Lahanmi 72
Lamido 33
Lateral Thinking 8
Lekki British International School 115
Lemo 76
Loyola College, Ibadan 90,137
Loyola Jesuit, Abuja 115
M
Mabogunje 36
Macaulay 21,22
Makinde, Yetunde 89,100
Mary Slessor 28
Mason, Donald Leslie 53
Mamora 34
Mayflower School Ikenne 93
Meadow Hall Schools 115

Mbadiwe 20, 28
Mbanefo 52
Meshida 69,87
Methodist Boys High School, Lagos 25
Methodist Boys High School, Oron 29
Methodist Girls High School, Ifaki 99
Methodist Girls High School, Lagos 27
Mindset 11
Momoh, John 20
Mohammed, Murtala 40
Murray-Bruce 48
N
Njoku 28,37 Raymond 48
Nigerian Turkish International College, Abuja 115
Norwegia International School, Port Harcourt 115
O
Obasanjo 7
Obi Peter 52
Obiano 52
Odedeji 8
Odili 52
Odutola 34
Offa Grammar School 77
Ogbe 33
Ogundipe, Phoebean 42
Ogunkua, Segun Babaijo 69
Ogunlade, R.A. 54,55,62
Ogunlesi 22, 32
Ogunleye, Oyinda 86
Ogunro, Sesan 70
Ogunwusi, Ooni 91
Owhatana 149
Ojukwu 33

Oke, Patrick 48
Okeke, Archbishop 52
Okigbo - Chris 46, Pius 52
Oko, Anya 28
Okogie, Olubunmi 47
Okoi, Arikpo 46
Okonjo-Iwela, Ngozi 104
Okotie, Chris 74
Okoya-Thomas 20
Oladitan 36, Yinka 49
Olashore International School, Iloko 115
Olashore, Oladele 77
Olatawura 55,68
Olivet Baptist High School 79
Olloh, Obi 74
Olubowale 9
Olubummo, Yewande 104
Olukoya 27
Olunloyo 44
Omolewa 69
Omotunde 99
Onabanjo 20
Onafowokan 30
Ondo Boys High School 37
Oni – Bolanle 78, Remi 78
Oputa 52
Orebe 11
Oron 29
Osadebay 28
Osanyinbi 23
Osibo 70
Osinbajo 50
Osoba 26
Osundare 11,69
Osuntokun – Jide 68, Kayode 68

Oteh, 10
Our Lady of the Apostles, Lagos 81
Owolabi - Ayodele 22, Israel 68
Oyawoye 77
Oyebode – Akin11,69 Femi69 Gbenga70
Oyebolu 43, 44
Oyekan 33
Oyeleke, Soji 78
Oyeyipo, Soji 78
P
Primary School Enrolment in 1955 185
Principals of Christ's School 63-65
Principals of Ifaki Grammar School 127-129
Pelly, Rosa Jane 97
Peterside 9, 33
Popoola, Tayo 78
Premium Institutions 17
Price, Bryan 9
Private schools 17
Q
Quadrangle 145
Qua Iboe Mission
Queen's College, Lagos 15, 41
Queen's School, Ibadan 86
R
Ransome-Kuti - Beko 30, Funmilayo 30
Reagan Memorial Baptist Girls School 73
Reminiscences of Alumni 137-1731
S
Saint Anne 24
Sanusi 33
Saraki – Bukola 33, Olusola 35
Saro-Wiwa 46
Securities and Exchange Commission 10

Shagari 40
Shenbanjo 10,22
Shobanjo 8
Shonekan 22
Sijuade 30
Slattery Rev Father 95
Sofola 35
Solanke 2
Solarin, Tai 93,94
Sonariwo 26
Soyinka 30,44
St Gregory 47
St Finbarr 95
St Thomas Aquinas College, Akure 84,
137
Sultan Abubakar 40
T
Tamuno, Tekena 87
Taylor, Ajibola 68
Timeline of landmarks in Christ's School
57-62
Titcombe College 83
U
Udo Udoma 72
Uganda 15
Umeadi 52
Unequal investment in education chart
186
Urhobo College, Effurum 87
Usman, Shamsudeen 33
Utomi, Patrick 52,91
V
Victor Uwaifo 48
W
Wabara 26

Wachukwu, Jaja 46
Wedmore 24
Wey 28
Williams - Akintola 22, Fatai 26 Funso 48
Y
Yar'Adua 40
Yuguda 10
Z
Zaria 39

ABOUT THE AUTHOR

Seye Adetunmbi is the Chief Responsibility Officer of Value Investing Limited, a portfolio management and financial advisory services company. He worked at various times as a consultant to Databank Zambia Limited, Department for International Development, United Kingdom and PYXERA Global. He is a prolific writer and the author of books which include: Applied Knowledge and Lateral Thinking, Like He That Serveth, Financial Intermediation and Practice, The School: A Compendium on Christ's School, Ado-Ekiti, Ekitipanupo Legacy Book, Christianity and Anglicanism, Mindset, The Apostle of Harmony, Atokeibeirosi: The Paradigm Shift Imperatives for an enduring Good Governance and Abridged Biographies & Panegyrics. He established Mindscope Africa, a publishing business concern, towards building commercial activities around his passion.

Seye is a product of Christ's School, Ado-Ekiti, University of Ilorin and University of Lagos, and he holds B. Sc. and MBA. He is a Fellow of the Chartered Institute of Stockbrokers and the Convener of Capital Market Roundtable in Nigeria. He also convened Ekitipanupo Forum, an Indigenous intellectual roundtable. His in-depth multidimensional writings on culture, tradition and history of his people has placed him as a consummate cultural anthropologist while his composite book on biographies underscores his resourcefulness as a tested historiographer.